Negro Higher Education in the 1960's

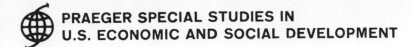

PRAEGER SPECIAL STUDIES IN
U.S. ECONOMIC AND SOCIAL DEVELOPMENT

Negro Higher Education in the 1960's

A. J. Jaffe
Walter Adams
Sandra G. Meyers

FREDERICK A. PRAEGER, Publishers
New York · Washington · London

The purpose of the Praeger Special Studies is to make specialized research monographs in U.S. and international economics and politics available to the academic, business, and government communities. For further information, write to the Special Projects Division, Frederick A. Praeger, Publishers, 111 Fourth Avenue, New York, N.Y. 10003.

FREDERICK A. PRAEGER, PUBLISHERS
111 Fourth Avenue, New York, N.Y. 10003, U.S.A.
5 Cromwell Place, London S.W. 7, England

Published in the United States of America in 1968
by Frederick A. Praeger, Inc., Publishers

PREFACE

This book is concerned, for the most part, with Southern primarily Negro colleges and with the students who attend them. The survey data we gathered are almost exclusively related to these two topics. We have extended our inquiry to some other areas of Negro higher education, using information from research other than our own, but this larger frame of reference serves principally to place the Negro colleges and their students in better perspective.

The study deals with a single racial minority group. As our findings emerged, and as we compared them with those from studies of other minority populations, we began to feel that many minority populations have substantially the same problems as the Southern Negro in securing a higher education of reasonable quality, and probably for many of the same reasons. We believe that many of our findings and comments apply to some other disadvantaged minorities in the United States--Mexican Americans, Puerto Ricans, isolated or impoverished white groups, American Indians, and many Negroes in the North and West.

The Southern Negro is in a unique position with respect to higher education because there are colleges readily available which have been established expressly for him. In many instances these colleges attempt to offer special services to meet his specific educational needs, in addition to a general college education. Our study attempts to evaluate the activities of these primarily Negro colleges in relation to the more general problem of higher education for disadvantaged minorities, and to determine the degree of their success or failure.

The U.S. Office of Education published somewhat similar studies of the primarily Negro
colleges as of 1930 and 1940. These earlier
studies were limited almost entirely to description, and took for granted the inevitability of
separate Negro colleges. No questions were raised
concerning the permanence of these schools, and no
mention was made of higher educational alternatives for the students. In the social context
of the period these omissions are hardly sur-
prising.

Our study is also descriptive, but in this
instance description serves as the basis for
evaluations and attempts at prediction. We repeatedly raise a number of questions, either ex-
plicitly stated or implicit in our presentation.
Why should separate Negro colleges exist? Will
they continue to exist in the future, and if so,
to what extent? How good are these colleges, and
for what kinds of lives do they prepare their
students? Why do the students attend them--
through preference or necessity, or for both
reasons? These questions reflect the issues and
conflicts of our day. The Negro's demand for
racial equality has had its broadest expression
in the battle for civil rights, but its most
dramatic, and frequently violent, expression has
been the struggle for integration of the nation's
schools.

The Supreme Court ruled in favor of integration, Congress enacted the enabling laws, and
agencies such as the Office of Education attempt
to implement them. If progress toward integration
has been slow and compromise frequent, the essential point remains that a clear position has been
taken and a course of action adopted. In spite of
determined opposition, social forces appear to be
moving toward the eventual abolition of separate
white and Negro schools. In this perspective the
primarily Negro colleges seem something of an

anachronism, and one might expect to find such
institutions playing a progressively less significant role in Negro education. Legal imperatives
for integration in higher education are perhaps
less compelling than in the case of the public
school system, but nevertheless there are strong
pressures for integrating the nation's colleges.

However, throughout the 1950's and 1960's
the primarily Negro colleges have continued their
long and virtually uninterrupted historical
growth. In the very recent past, when one might
least anticipate it, the rate of that growth has
substantially increased. Steadily mounting numbers of essentially the same kinds and qualities
of students enter these colleges today as entered
them a quarter century and more in the past.

We have tried to identify some of the
factors which have influenced this continuing
growth, and the factors working for and against
the separate Negro college. We urge the reader
to review the entire body of evidence, and then
judge for himself the future possibilities.
Furthermore, since we have not attempted to
summarize the very large body of literature on
this subject, we wish to remind the reader to
take into account this vast outpouring. In particular, attention is directed to a classic report (although published only in 1965), Earl J.
McGrath's The Predominantly Negro College in
Transition.* We also wish to call attention to
a study of the students of fifty primarily Negro
colleges just following graduation, which was
published too late for consideration in our
analysis, Graduates of Predominantly Negro

_____

*Earl J. McGrath, The Predominantly Negro
College in Transition (New York: Teachers College,
Columbia University, 1965).

Colleges, Class of 1964 by Joseph H. Fichter.* It
was prepared for the National Institutes of Health,
with joint sponsorship by the U.S. Department of
Labor and the National Science Foundation. The
study not only supports many of our own findings,
particularly those concerning occupational plans
and plans for graduate education, but also con-
siders in greater depth than our research the
various factors relevant to these plans.

Chapter 1 consists of introductory observations on the significance of primarily Negro
colleges, a brief discussion of the objectives of
the study, and a description of the study design.
In Chapter 2 are presented some historical
materials on Negro colleges and their students
during the past third of a century. The procedures by which students are brought into the
Negro college system are described in Chapter 3,
as well as recent trends in applicants, new entrants, and total enrollments. Chapter 4 deals
with the new entrants themselves, the Southern
Negro high school seniors planning on college.
The 1965 Negro college students are described in
Chapter 5. Chapter 6 assesses the realism of
their post-college plans--their occupational
aspirations, plans for post-graduate and professional study, and desired region of future
residence. Chapter 7 presents data on the extent
of social class differences between students
attending Negro colleges of varying quality, and
on differences in the academic prowess of the
students. We discuss the small minority of the
colleges which attract the elite students--
students who have both markedly superior academic

---

*Joseph H. Fichter, Graduates of Predominantly
Negro Colleges, Class of 1964 (Washington, D.C.:
U.S. Government Printing Office, Public Health
Service Publication No. 1571, 1967).

performance and socio-economic advantages, relative to other students. In Chapter 8 we consider
the role of the public junior college in Negro
higher education, both in the South and elsewhere.
The relative importance of this type of school
for Negro and white students is discussed, and an
attempt is made to forecast future availability
of public junior colleges in the South. Projected numbers of Southern Negro high school
graduates' in 1975, the future candidates for the
Negro colleges, are presented state by state in
Chapter 9. Chapter 10 summarizes the salient
findings, and their implications, as we perceive
them, for educational policies and programs.

For reading convenience the basic statistical tables are assembled in Appendix A, and the
survey methodology is detailed in Appendix B.
Appendix C offers additional notes on the quality
ratings for the primarily Negro colleges, and a
comparison with another recent quality index of
these colleges. Appendices D and E, in effect,
are extended footnotes to Chapters 4 and 9, respectively. Appendix D reviews past and recent
research findings concerning the relative academic standings of white and Negro youth, students and nonstudents. Appendix E consists of
additional projections to 1975--estimates of
numbers of Southern Negro youth at that date at
three levels of educational attainment.

ACKNOWLEDGMENTS

Our thanks are extended to the many college
and high school administrators and students who
took the time and effort necessary to answer our
questionnaires. In ordinary times people are
often pleased to answer questions about themselves. But these are not ordinary times. When
they received our enquiries the Negro colleges
and high schools were already being bombarded by

requests for assistance from a variety of private and government-sponsored surveys. That they even bothered with ours speaks well for their cooperative attitudes.

Of the people who gave us advice and counsel, we are especially indebted to S. A. Kendrick, Executive Associate of the College Entrance Examination Board. We also wish to express our gratitude to that organization, whose financial support made this study possible.

Dr. Stephen S. Wright, formerly President of Fisk University, and currently President of the United Negro College Fund, reviewed the initial mimeographed version of this study. His suggestions and criticisms led to many of the revisions and additions incorporated in the present volume.

Our thanks are extended to Dr. Sydney S. Spivack of Princeton University, whose suggestions and contributions to our study were invaluable.

William T. Allen, Jr., now Assistant Director of Admissions at Yale University, was instrumental in converting the considerable number of diverse educational tests into a uniform rating system for use in our analysis.

The personnel of the Southern Regional Office of the College Entrance Examination Board provided welcome assistance, especially in obtaining responses from educational institutions.

And to Mrs. J. Miles we extend our thanks for her valiant editorial assistance.

A. J. Jaffe
Walter Adams
Sandra G. Meyers

December, 1967

CONTENTS

Page

PREFACE   v

LIST OF CHARTS   xix

LIST OF TABLES   xxiii

Chapter

1   INTRODUCTION   3

        Study Design   5
        Quality Ratings of Negro Colleges   7

2   SOME HISTORICAL TRENDS   8

        Integration Versus Separation--
            Then and Now   9
        Trends in Enrollment   11
            Trends in High School Graduation   11
            Trends in College Entrance   13
            Trends in Enrollment in Negro
                Colleges   14
        The Students   16
            Personal Characteristics   17
            Job Plans   17
            Educational Preparation   17
            Major Area of Study   19
            Socio-Economic Background   21
        Conclusions   21
        Notes   22

Chapter   Page

3   RECRUITMENT PRACTICES   24

        Applicants, Admissions, and
            Enrollments   25
                Applicants   25
                Acceptance and Entry   27
                Changes in Enrollment   28
                    1962-1965   28
                        Estimated 1968 Enrollment   32
            Recruitment of Students   32
            Criteria for Student Admissions   34
            Student Financing   36
            Some Questions   39
            Notes   42

4   FROM HIGH SCHOOL SENIOR TO COLLEGE
        FRESHMAN   44

            Proportion Going to College   45
            Negro or Integrated College?   46
            Location of College   49
            Academic Rating of College Entrants
                and Type of College Entered   50
                Ranking of Students   50
                The Students with Test-Score
                    Ranking   50
                The Students without Test-
                    Score Ranking   53
                The Colleges   54
            Location of High School in Relation
                to Quality and Type of College
                Entered   55
            Sex Distribution of the College
                Entrants   56
            Characteristics Related to High
                Schools and Colleges   57
            Notes   58

Chapter   Page

5   THE COLLEGE STUDENTS   60

        Social and Economic Background   61
        Region of Origin and Future Hopes   62
        Scholastic Characteristics   62
        Occupational Plans   65
        High School Standing   68
        Financing of College   68
        Personal Characteristics   69
        Notes   69

6   ASPIRATIONS AND REALITY   71

        Backgrounds and Goals   73
        Completing Four Years of College   74
        Attending Graduate School   76
        Occupational Choice   77
            The Students' Beliefs   77
            The College Graduates   79
            The College Dropouts   81
            Teaching   81
        Will They Leave the South?   84
        Notes   87

7   COLLEGES AND SOCIAL CLASS   90

        Class Differences in College
          Enrollment   91
        Class Differences among the Negro
          Colleges   92
            Academic Abilities of Students   92
            Social Class   93
            Geographic Origin   95
        Student Aspirations   96
        Conclusions   96
        Notes   97

Chapter   Page

  8   THE SOUTHERN NEGRO COLLEGE STUDENT
      AND PUBLIC JUNIOR COLLEGES   98

         Growth of the Two-Year College   99
         Who Goes to Junior Colleges?   101
         The Public Junior Colleges   104
         Availability and Negro Enrollment   106
         Possible Expansion of Public
            Junior Colleges in the South   110
         Public Junior Colleges and the
            Four-Year Negro College   112
         Notes   114

  9   PROJECTIONS TO 1975 OF HIGH SCHOOL
      GRADUATES BY STATES   117

         Notes   121

 10   MAJOR FINDINGS AND THEIR POLICY
      IMPLICATIONS   122

         The Findings   123
            Growth in Enrollment   123
            The Students   124
            The Colleges   126
         Implications and Recommendations   128
            The Colleges   129
               Public Junior and
                  "Poor" Negro Colleges   129
               The High Quality
                  Colleges   132
            The Students   132
               The Able College
                  Entrants   132
               The Poorly Prepared
                  College Entrants   134
            Pre-College Education   134
         Notes   138

Appendix   Page

A   STATISTICAL TABLES   143

    Notes on the Data and the
        Tabulations   143

B   METHODOLOGY   183

    Determining Long-Run Trends in
        Educational Attainment   183
    The Three Questionnaire Surveys   186
        I. Survey of Students in
            Primarily Negro Colleges   187
            General Description of
                Survey   187
            The Survey Universe   188
            Sampling from the Uni-
                verse of Primarily
                Negro Colleges   189
            Sampling from the
                Students Enrolled
                in the Sixty-Eight
                Colleges   195
            Limitations of the Data   197
            Negro Students in
                Southern Integrated
                Colleges   199
            Completeness and Quality
                of the Questionnaire
                Responses   200
        II. Survey of Southern Negro
            High School Graduates
            Planning on College
            Entrance in Fall, 1965
            (Excluding Graduates from
            the Border States)   201
            General Description of
                Survey   201
            The Survey Universe   202

Appendix   Page

                Sampling from the
                  Initial Universe of
                  Negro High Schools   203
                Estimated Probable
                  Universe   205
                Further Comparisons
                  Between the Sample
                  of Fifty and the
                  Larger Sample   205
                Completeness and Quality
                  of the Questionnaire
                  Responses   211

         III. Survey of Negro College
                Enrollments, Student
                Recruitment and Admissions,
                and Student Financing   214
                General Description of
                  Survey   214
                The Survey Universe   215
                Returns from the Survey
                  Universe   217
                Completeness and Quality
                  of the Questionnaire
                  Responses   222
         IV. The Major Problems for the
                Three Surveys   223
                The Reluctant Respondents   223
                The Problem of Obtaining
                  Test-Score Data for the
                  Primarily Negro College
                  Students   227
          V. General Evaluation of the
                Surveys   228

  C   NOTES ON COLLEGE QUALITY RATINGS   233

     Introduction   233
     Original Ratings by Experts   234
     1967 Ratings   238
     The Elite Colleges   240

Appendix   Page

D   PAST AND PRESENT TEST PERFORMANCE   245

    Introduction   245
    Some Findings of the Office of
      Education Study   246
    Armed Forces Tests   250
        World War I   251
        Draftees, 1964-1965   251
    Notes   253

E   PROJECTED EDUCATIONAL ATTAINMENT
    OF SOUTHERN NEGRO YOUTH   257

    Findings   257
    Some Implications   259
    Methodology of the Projections   262
        Sources of Data   262
        General Procedures   263
        Projecting Numbers of High
          School Entrants   264
        Projecting Numbers of High
          School Graduates   268
        Projections of Numbers
          Completing at Least One
          Year of College   268
    Summary   270
    Notes   272

F   SURVEY QUESTIONNAIRES   275

BIBLIOGRAPHY OF TEXT REFERENCES   287

ABOUT THE AUTHORS   291

LIST OF CHARTS

Chart   Page

2.1   Enrollment in Thirty-Six Negro
      Accredited Colleges, 1910-1963   15

3.1   Distribution of Students Enrolled
      in Four-Year Primarily Negro
      Colleges, 1965, by Quality of
      College   26

3.2   Per Cent Increase in New Entrants
      to Four-Year Primarily Negro
      Colleges, 1962-1965, by Quality
      of College and Location of
      College   29

4.1   Distribution of All Spring, 1965,
      Southern Negro High School
      Seniors Planning on Entering
      Different Types, Qualities,
      and Locations of College   48

4.2   Distribution of Spring, 1965,
      Southern Negro High School
      Seniors Planning on College
      by High School and National
      Test-Score Standing   51

Chart   Page

4.3   Distribution of Southern Negro
        High School Seniors, Spring,
        1965, Planning on Entering
        College, by National Test-
        Score Standing and Type of
        College   52

5.1   Distribution of Students by
        Quality of College, 1965, and
        by Location of High School
        and of College   63

5.2   Distribution of Students by
        Quality of College, 1965,
        and Occupational Choice   66

7.1   Comparison of Students at Elite
        Versus "Poor" Colleges,
        Selected Characteristics   94

8.1   Total National Enrollment in
        Two-Year Public Colleges,
        1920-1965   100

8.2   Attendance at and Availability
        of Junior Colleges, by Region   108

        (a)   Proportions of All Negro
              and White Degree-Credit
              Undergraduates Enrolled
              in College Who Were
              Attending Public Junior
              Colleges, by Region,
              October, 1965   108

        (b)   Number of Public Junior
              Colleges, 1965, by
              Region, and for
              Selected States   108

Chart   Page

E.1   Southern Nonwhite Population
       Eighteen to Twenty-Four Years
       of Age, 1940-1960, and Pro-
       jected for 1975   260

E.2   Number of Southern Nonwhite Youth
       Eighteen to Twenty-Four Years
       of Age Who Completed at Least
       the First Year of High School,
       1940-1960, and Projected for
       1975   265

E.3   Number of Southern Nonwhite Youth
       Eighteen to Twenty-Four Years
       of Age Who Completed High
       School or More, 1940-1960, and
       Projected for 1975   269

E.4   Number of Southern Nonwhite Youth
       Eighteen to Twenty-Four Years
       of Age Who Completed at Least
       the First Year of College,
       1940-1960, and Projected for
       1975   271

LIST OF TABLES

Page

Appendix A

1   Quality, type, and location of
    college by changes in total
    enrollment, 1962, 1965, and
    expected for 1968   146

2   Per cent increase in new entrants,
    1962-1965, by quality of college
    and location of college   147

3   Quality of college by per cent
    increases in new applicants,
    applicants accepted, and
    acceptances in fact entering
    colleges, 1962-1965   148

4   Quality of college by proportions
    of colleges which have a full-
    time recruitment person or a
    person for whom recruitment is
    an important part of the
    official job   149

5   Quality of college by reasons
    given for expansion of recruit-
    ment program in the next three
    years   150

Page

6   Proportions of colleges of differ-
     ent qualities especially anxious
     to enroll particular types or
     groups of students   151

7   Quality of college by the one most
     important criterion for the
     student admission decision   152

8   Quality of college by proportions
     of students receiving financial
     aid of various kinds   153

9   Type and location of college
     entered by location of high
     school from which graduated
     in Spring, 1965   154

10   Test-score ranking of students by
     location of high school and
     type and location of college
     entered   155

11   Number in high school graduating
     class, by location of high
     school, by per cent distribu-
     tion of test-score ranking of
     students   156

12   Number of college entrants by
     location of high school by per
     cent distribution of test-score
     ranking of students   157

13   Per cent distribution of size of
     college entered, by location of
     high school and test-score
     ranking of students   158

Page

14   Occupational distribution of
      Southern nonwhite males, and
      of the fathers of students, by
      type and quality of college   159

15   Labor force status and occupational
      distribution for the mothers of
      students, by type and quality of
      college   160

16   Years of schooling completed for
      Southern nonwhite males, and for
      the fathers of students, by type
      and quality of college   161

17   Years of schooling completed for
      Southern nonwhite females, and
      for the mothers of students, by
      type and quality of college   162

18   Income distribution for Southern
      nonwhite families, and for the
      student's immediate household,
      by type and quality of college   163

19   Family income distribution for
      students in primarily Negro
      colleges, and for all U.S.
      college students   164

20   Distribution by location of high
      school from which student
      graduated, by type and quality
      of college   165

21   Location of college by location
      of high school from which
      student graduated, by type and
      quality of college   166

Page

22 Desired region of residence after
    finishing college, by type and
    quality of college   167

23 Distribution by major field of
    study, by type and quality of
    college   168

24 Selected scholastic characteristics
    of students, by type and quality
    of college   170

25 Expected major occupational group
    after finishing college, by type
    and quality of college   171

26 Expected specific occupations for
    students who intend to be pro-
    fessional workers, by type and
    quality of college   172

27 Distribution of students by
    standing in high school class,
    by type and quality of college   173

28 Number and sources of student
    financing, by type and quality
    of college   174

29 Sex, age, and marital status of
    students, by type and quality
    of college   175

30 Year in college and residence
    arrangements of students, by
    type and quality of college   176

31 Number and sources of encouragement
    to students to enter college, by
    type and quality of college   177

Page

32   Rates of out-migration from the
      South, nonwhites, by age, sex,
      and education, 1955-1960   178

33   Per cent distribution of major
      occupation groups by education,
      color, and sex, persons twenty-
      five years of age and over,
      United States, 1960   179

34   Percentage distribution of college
      graduates in teaching and other
      occupations, by color and sex,
      United States, 1960   180

Appendix B

B.1   Proportions graduating from high
      school, college entrants, and
      college graduates, by sex and
      color: United States, about 1875
      to 1955   184

B.2   Numbers of colleges by type,
      enrollment size, and size of
      community   191

Appendix E

E.1   Distribution by years of schooling
      completed, of Southern nonwhite
      youth aged eighteen to twenty-
      four, 1960 and projected 1975
      estimates   258

E.2   Methodology for making 1975 pro-
      jections of educational attain-
      ment of Southern nonwhite youth
      aged eighteen to twenty-four   266

Negro Higher
Education
in the 1960's

CHAPTER **1** INTRODUCTION

In the mid-1960's there were over one hundred primarily Negro colleges located mainly in the South, designated by the U.S. Office of Education as such, and so recognized by the institutions themselves. Over 100,000 students, slightly more than half of all American Negro college students, attended these colleges. In 1950, as nearly as can be estimated, some 60 per cent of the Negro college students were enrolled in Negro colleges. Precise figures for both dates are not available, but that there was a decrease in recent years is clear.

This decrease in the proportion of all Negro college youth attending primarily Negro colleges may be attributed to a number of factors. One is the large volume of out-migration from the South. The Negro graduate from a Northern or Western high school is much more likely to attend a local college than to move to the South to attend a Negro college. Thus, over the years, and partly as a result of this out-migration, more Negro students have enrolled in primarily white Northern and Western colleges, both two- and four-year institutions.

Another reason is the recent increase in public two-year colleges in a number of Southern states. These schools are officially integrated, and hence excluded from any statistics of "primarily Negro colleges." A third reason, and statistically least important, is the increasing attendance of Negroes in primarily white four-year colleges in the South. Altogether, these three factors have led a decreasing proportion of all Negro college students to enroll in the primarily Negro colleges.

Nevertheless, the total number of Negroes attending these colleges has steadily increased in recent years, due to increasing population and numbers of high school graduates, and in the last few years this increase has apparently accelerated. The expansion has kept pace with that of all colleges in this country. We may assume that in the foreseeable future the enrollment at Negro colleges will continue to increase. The Southern Negro college is still the most important higher educational opportunity available to Southern Negro youth.

There is ample reason, then, to ask: What kinds of students enter these colleges, and what kinds and qualities of colleges are they entering? It is important to know just how rapidly the primarily Negro colleges are expanding. Are the academically better or the poorer of these schools expanding most swiftly? Are there particular subregions of the South where such expansion is particularly pronounced? And finally, how many Negro high school graduates might there be in the South in 1975?

In order to answer these questions, particularly those involving quality of college, we should have comparable information for the white--or integrated--colleges both in the South and elsewhere. By comparing the Negro colleges with the others, we could obtain a much better perspective and understanding of the former. Unfortunately, however, the scope of our study made it impractical to obtain parallel data for white colleges and comparisons of the two types of colleges cannot be drawn.

STUDY DESIGN*

The research consisted essentially of three interrelated surveys, all conducted in the latter half of 1965 and the first half of 1966, plus the preparation of projections to 1975. Additional existing data supplemented the information we collected.

1) In order to determine characteristics of students attending primarily Negro colleges in 1965, student questionnaires were distributed at a sample of the universe of these colleges. The essential information obtained consisted of the socio-economic background of the students--such as education and occupation of parents and family income--plus the personal characteristics of the students themselves--academic achievement, subject of major interest, occupational and future residence plans, and so forth.

2) A second, briefer questionnaire was sent to Southern Negro high schools, excepting those in the border states, requesting information on the Spring, 1965, graduates who expected to enter college the following Fall. In addition to sex and class rank, we asked for aptitude and achievement test scores in order to determine how the college entrants compared to high school students throughout the country. We also obtained information about the high school, such as its location, the size of the graduating class, and numbers and proportions going on to college, plus information about the colleges the students were entering.

The two samples of college students and college entrants supplemented each other, the college

---

*More details on the methodology are presented in Appendix B.

student sample affording greater detail on student characteristics, and the college entrant sample permitting comparison of students entering integrated versus primarily Negro colleges, and colleges in and out of the South.

3) A third questionnaire was addressed to officials of the four-year Negro colleges and sought information for each school on recent and projected trends in applicants, acceptances, new entrants, and total enrollments; trends in practices and plans regarding recruitment of students; admissions policies and preferences; and specific data on funds available to students for financing their college expenses. With such information, we were better able to relate characteristics of the colleges to characteristics of the students attending or entering them. In this survey we did not select a sample from the four-year colleges, but attempted to obtain a completed questionnaire from each school. We did so because the respondent unit in this case was the college, and the total number of colleges was small.

4) We developed projections to 1975 for fourteen Southern states of the numbers of Southern Negro youth expected to be high school graduates. Our belief was that the findings from our three questionnaires would have greater or lesser significance precisely to the extent that the population of Southern Negro high school graduates increased, since they are the candidates for entry to primarily Negro colleges.

5) In addition to the data we collected, we reviewed a considerable body of existing information, both current and historical, relevant to Negro college students, the colleges they attend, and relationships between higher education and life goals for these students. Prominent among these data are statistics collected by the Office

of Education, the Bureau of the Census, and a number of university-affiliated social research institutes.

QUALITY RATINGS OF NEGRO COLLEGES

A large part of the analysis focuses on three quality groups of the four-year Negro colleges. The two-year schools are not rated and are always shown separately, since they are too different in objectives and offerings for inclusion with four-year colleges.

Our three quality groups are "good," "fair," and "poor" colleges. The ratings were made in the early 1960's by six authorities on primarily Negro colleges, each expert independently scoring each college on a scale from 0 to 3. The final rating of a college was the average of the separate ratings. Since the conclusions we reach from our analysis of the quality groups of colleges are not optimistic ones, and may well prove controversial, we present in Appendix C a more detailed discussion of the quality index we used and the problems associated with such ratings in general.

We also analyzed separately those few colleges which enroll students of unusually high academic calibre, relative to students at all other Negro colleges, in order to determine whether the academically elite students also differed in other respects, such as background characteristics, geographical origins, and occupational aspirations. In Appendix C we describe the manner in which we identified these few highly selective colleges.

CHAPTER SOME
HISTORICAL
TRENDS

1) *Since the latter part of the nineteenth century, between 4 and 5 out of every
10 male Negro high school graduates, and a
slightly smaller proportion of females, have
entered college. The large increase in
Negro college enrollment since World War II
has resulted mainly from the fact that
larger numbers have completed high school.*

2) *Enrollment in primarily Negro colleges in the South increased very greatly
between 1910 and 1965, from a very few
thousand to over 100,000.*

3) *The characteristics of the students
have changed little, if at all, over the
last generation or longer.*

    a) *There were more women
       students than men.*

    b) *Most graduated from a
       Southern high school.*

    c) *About half expected to
       become teachers.*

> d) *The majority of the*
>   *students have always*
>   *come from relatively*
>   *high socio-economic*
>   *backgrounds (in com-*
>   *parison with all*
>   *Southern Negro youth).*
>
> e) *The large majority*
>   *were in the bottom*
>   *half of national test-*
>   *score distributions.*

INTEGRATION VERSUS SEPARATION--
THEN AND NOW

In many ways the 1960's recapitulate the experience of Negroes in the immediate post-Civil War
years. At that time also, just after the abolition
of slavery, equalitarian forces were dominant. The
former slave emerged as a citizen with voting and
other political rights. The impact of the Thir-
teenth and Fourteenth Constitutional Amendments,
plus the efforts of individuals and of agencies
such as the Freedmen's Bureau, led to more than a
decade of increasingly equal rights. But this was
also the period when extensive efforts, and considerable public and private moneys, were expended
on the establishment of numerous separate Negro
institutes and colleges. The foundations were laid
for an enduring segregated Negro higher educational
establishment at precisely the time when most other
racial barriers were under heavy attack.

Two facts should be kept in mind if we wish to
understand what occurred in Negro education just
after the Civil War, and what is apparently
occurring today. In both periods large numbers of
Negroes, newly aware of their civil rights,
actively sought to obtain them, with the aid and
encouragement of influential liberals. Education
was one of these rights. Both then and today

Negroes who sought advanced education generally
lacked the educational base needed to enter the
same courses of schooling as their white contem-
poraries.

Prior to the Civil War, formal education of
most Southern Negroes was prohibited by law.
Given this fact, it would have been quite unrealistic for the post-Civil War reformers to attempt
to integrate Negroes into the white educational
complex except for young children beginning their
elementary school education, and there is evidence
that this possibility was seldom seriously considered. The establishment of separate Negro
schools, institutes, and colleges seemed the practical way to meet the educational needs of the
newly emancipated population. When the reaction
to post-war liberalism set in late in the century,
these schools and colleges represented virtually
the only educational opportunity for Southern
Negroes, and have endured and expanded down the
years.

A similar situation exists today during the
second great historical movement for racial
equality. Southern primary and secondary schools,
still largely segregated, as well as "ghetto
schools" in the North and West, continue their
historical failure to give Negro children the academic level of attainment most white children
enjoy. The generally deprived backgrounds of the
Negro children emerge as severe handicaps in the
educational process, handicaps which their schools
fail to surmount. The primarily Negro college
thus remains the most accessible form of higher
education for Southern Negro high school graduates
because they rely principally on the high school
record of the candidate, rather than on his
national standing on academic tests. The high
school record measures preparation relative to the
rest of the high school class, and so does not
work to the disadvantage of students from less
adequate high schools. Moreover, many of the

Negro colleges, aware of the problem of poor preparation of their entrants, offer special courses
of remedial work.

There are, of course, other factors favoring
the continuing prominence of the primarily Negro
colleges. They are relatively inexpensive schools,
a point of considerable importance to an economically deprived minority. Also, the Negro student
in a primarily white college necessarily experiences considerable, no doubt painful, social isolation. But these problems, we feel, are relatively more amenable to change than is the enduring
academic one of inadequate preparation, rooted as
it is in the child's total educational experience
throughout the primary and secondary school years.

TRENDS IN ENROLLMENT

The findings which follow derive from an
analysis of the educational attainment of the
several age cohorts of Negro students as reported
in the U.S. decennial censuses of 1940 and 1960.[1]
Since the students in these Negro colleges are a
major fraction of all Negro college students, the
growth of these colleges is closely related to
growth in numbers and proportions of the total
Negro population completing high school and
entering college.

Trends in High School Graduation

Down the years a much smaller proportion of
the nonwhite population, both men and women, than
of the white, has graduated from high school. In
the period just after the Civil War, perhaps only
2 to 3 per cent of the *nonwhite men* had graduated
from high school. The proportion increased gradually over the decades, and 39 per cent of those
aged twenty to twenty-four in 1960 reported having

finished twelve years of school. (These people were of high school graduation age around 1955.)

Among the *nonwhite women*, the levels of--and trends in--high school graduation were very simi-lar to those of the nonwhite men. However, the data suggest that during the late nineteenth cen-tury a slightly larger proportion of the men may have graduated from high school, whereas during the twentieth century a slightly larger proportion of the nonwhite women may have graduated. Of women aged twenty to twenty-four in 1960, 45 per cent had completed twelve years of school, as com-pared with 39 per cent for the men.

Among *white men* the proportion who graduated from high school increased from about 10 per cent in the period around 1880 to over 60 per cent in 1960. There does not appear to be any particular period within this time span in which one could say for certain that the rate of high school graduation was increasing unusually rapidly or slowly.

Among *white women* we find practically the same trend. However, in each time period a slightly larger proportion of the women than of the men graduated from high school. For example, among white women aged twenty to twenty-four in 1960, 68 per cent had graduated from high school, as compared with 65 per cent of white men.

As of about 1960, fewer than half of the non-whites of high school graduation age actually graduated from secondary school. In this respect nonwhites are about one generation behind white youngsters. Around 1930 about the same proportion of white teenagers had completed high school as had nonwhites around 1960. The numbers of non-whites who go to college, then, would of necessity be limited, since high school graduation is virtu-ally a standard entrance requirement. Many more

whites than Negroes are eligible to attend college
because more of them have finished secondary
school.

Since the end of World War II the proportion
of high school age nonwhites who completed high
school has gone up about one fifth.[2] This means
that more nonwhites may enter college, assuming
that other factors permit them to do so--financial
situation, space in the colleges, and so forth.

Trends in College Entrance

Among *nonwhite men* there was a long-time
decrease in the proportion of high school graduates who entered college. Around the turn of the
century and through World War I, about half
entered college. During the 1920's and 1930's,
the proportion fell, and today only some 4 in 10,
perhaps, of the high school graduates enter
college.

For *nonwhite women*, trends in college enrollment have been very similar to those for white
women. Around the turn of the century perhaps 40
per cent, or slightly more, of these high school
graduates enrolled in college. During the Depression the proportion gradually fell to a level
at which about 3 in 10 entered college.

Among *white men* about half of all those who
had graduated from high school entered college--
both two- and four-year institutions. Among the
cohorts which were of high school graduation age
from about 1880 to the middle of the 1920's, there
were only fluctuations around the 50 per cent mark.
We feel that these result from small differences
in the quality of the data rather than any true
changes in the propensity of high school graduates
to enroll in a college or university.

Some time during the middle or late 1920's, perhaps coincidentally with the onslaught of the Great Depression, the proportion of male white high school graduates going on to college dropped significantly. Of those who were of high school graduation age around 1935, only about 4 in 10 entered college. World War II also proved an obstacle to college entry. In effect, many of the men who might have entered college in the late 1930's or early 1940's apparently never did so. By 1945 we return to the historical pattern-- about half of high school graduates enter college.

The proportion of *white female* high school graduates who enter college seems to have hovered in the neighborhood of 40 per cent, or slightly over, during the period from 1880 to the middle or latter part of the 1920's. As with the men, the Great Depression of the 1930's resulted in a decrease in college going; during the 1930's and 1940's only about 30 per cent of white women high school graduates entered college.

Trends in Enrollment in Negro Colleges

The long-term increases in enrollment in primarily Negro colleges are indicated by data for thirty-six colleges--twenty of them private and sixteen public[3]--comprising about a third of all primarily Negro colleges (Chart 2.1). Each has had a consecutive existence since the early years of the present century, most were established during the last quarter of the nineteenth century, and all are accredited schools. They are the larger colleges in the universe of such institutions, and accounted for about two thirds of the students enrolled in primarily Negro colleges in 1963. These colleges, especially the public ones, have had steadily mounting enrollments for over half a century and into the mid-1960's.

Chart 2.1

Enrollment in Thirty-Six Negro
Accredited Colleges, 1910-1963

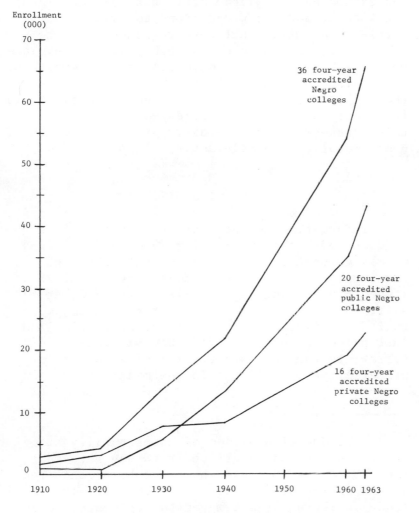

Enrollment
(000)

36 four-year
accredited
Negro
colleges

20 four-year
accredited
public Negro
colleges

16 four-year
accredited
private Negro
colleges

Sources: <u>General Studies of Colleges for Negroes</u>,
U.S. Office of Education, 1942, Table 1,
p. 4; and for the two recent years,
tabulated from Office of Education
higher education directories for the
identical colleges.

If long-time trends are any augur of what
lies ahead, it would seem that the primarily Negro
colleges will not only survive, but will continue
rapid expansion of their student enrollments. On
the basis of these historical and recent trends,
the estimates of college officials for the immediate future, and our projections to 1975, we have
little expectation that desegregation of white
colleges in the South or any other likely development, with the possible exception of the growth of
the public two-year college, will reduce greatly
the quantitative importance of the primarily Negro
four-year college in the foreseeable future. In
this perspective the characteristics of the students enrolled are relevant.

THE STUDENTS

Information on the characteristics of the
student body is available for 1930 and 1940, and
we may compare this information with our 1965
findings.[4] To what extent do the relatively few
students attending Negro colleges in 1930, at the
start of the Great Depression, resemble those enrolled in 1940, at the end of the Depression and
just prior to World War II? How similar, or different, is the far larger total of students in
primarily Negro colleges in the mid-1960's?[*]

---

[*]The question arises of comparability among
the three studies. Suffice it to say here that
the 1930 and 1940 researches were both conducted
by the Office of Education, and that the 1940
study deliberately attempted to duplicate, to the
extent possible, the earlier survey. Our own
student questionnaire was designed to include a
number of items of information in the earlier
studies. The samples for the three studies are
not identical, and we are skeptical of differences

The salient finding is that *students enrolled in 1930 and in 1965 closely resemble each other.*

Personal Characteristics

Fewer men than women attended the Negro colleges in 1930, 1940, and 1965, and changes in the proportions are insignificant. Both then and now there were about six women enrolled to four men. Whatever the survey date, between 8 and 9 of every 10 students had attended high school in the South.

Job Plans

In 1940 and 1965 about half of all students expected to become teachers following graduation. In 1940 and in 1965, more of the women than of the men were preparing to teach. In 1940, 9 out of 10 students expected to enter white-collar occupations, and by 1965 the only change was that this aspiration had become virtually unanimous.

Educational Preparation

The 1940 study attempted to relate the educational preparation of freshmen in primarily Negro colleges to that of all students in the United States. The instrument used was the American Council on Education Psychological Examination for College Freshmen, Form 1940. National norms had been established for this test, based on scores for about 72,000 freshmen

---

of a very few percentage points. The tables appear to confirm each other, however, and there are consecutive trends, or absences of trends, over the thirty-five year span of time.

in 374 colleges throughout the country. Exactly
how comparable the findings for this 1940 test
are to our 1965 findings we do not know; nevertheless, some inferences can be drawn from comparison
of the two sets of data. In the earlier study the
tests were administered to college freshmen; in
the 1965 study they were given to high school students. In the earlier study some small proportion
of the students tested had attended non-Southern
high schools. The 1965 data were limited to students attending Southern Negro high schools--the
great majority, but not the total universe, of
Negro college entrants. Furthermore, tests of
student aptitude or achievement are not the most
precise of measuring instruments, and we are certain that a 1940 test can be only very roughly
compared with the wide variety of tests given in
the 1960's.*

Nevertheless, the findings from the test
data, 1940 and 1965, agree on the one most general
conclusion: *Then and now the students rank well
below all students in the country in academic*

---

*We should also point out that in our sample
the 1965 students were the better ones, since they
were the ones who were planning on college; 75 per
cent of them were in the upper half of their high
school classes. The test scores of these Negro
students were compared with those for all students
who took these tests in high school--college candidates and noncandidates alike.

The 1940 data are based, for both Negro and
white students, on the test performance of all
college freshmen--presumably a high-ability population, relative to the total population tested
for the 1965 data. The 1965 Negro students'
relative performance accordingly should benefit
from this less rigorous comparison.

attainment. Three out of four of the 1965 Negro
college entrants ranked in the lower half of the
national test-score distribution. In 1940 the
Negro college freshman median score was at the
fourth percentile from the bottom of the national
distribution.

If the relative performance of the Negro students has somewhat improved, as these statistics
seem to suggest, the discrepancy remains a considerable one--certainly sufficient to represent
a severe handicap in the contest for entrance to
good colleges. The statistics for the two dates
are evidence of the salient point--that the
Southern Negro students since 1940 have been far
less prepared for college-level work than the universe of students, Negro and white, throughout the
country.*

In order to obtain a longer view of the
rankings in national test scores, we present in
Appendix D some materials taken from the experiences of the U.S. military forces at the time of
World War I. Admittedly the military recruits are
not comparable to the college-going population,
but any changes over time in the two groups of
youth should be approximately parallel, and thus
we were able to extend our information for college
youth over a half century.

Major Area of Study

It is only when we compare past and current
student majors that any significant changes seem
to have taken place. Between 1930 and 1965 the

---

*The findings from a 1965 Office of Education
study are also included in Appendix D; they confirm the conclusions from our own data.

proportion who were education majors nearly
doubled. Just under a third of all students were
education majors in 1965. Proportions majoring
in the physical sciences, and "all other" majors
(chiefly the humanities, such as art, music,
philosophy, and languages and literature) dropped
by about a third each. Proportions majoring in
the social and life sciences rose by about half,
as follows:

Proportion Enrolled in Each Major Field

Major	1930	1940	1965
	%	%	%
Physical sciences	29	25	20
Social and life sciences	13	20	22
All education	16	23	30
All other majors[a]	42	32	28
All majors	100	100	100

[a]Primarily the "humanities," such as art,
music, philosophy, and languages and literature.

Just why these changes occurred we do not
know. Since the proportion hoping to teach did
not change, perhaps a specific education major is
required more frequently today. Perhaps social
problems and issues, the essential content of the
social sciences, have increasingly engaged Negro
students as members of a disadvantaged minority.
Whatever the reasons may be, the changes are de-
scriptively interesting but have had little
apparent effect on occupational choice, to the
extent that choice can be ascertained.

Socio-Economic Background

Over the thirty-five years, the student body
has come from essentially the same family background. Whatever the survey date, there were
about the same proportions of fathers in each of
the broad occupational categories. About a
quarter were white-collar workers, and the large
majority of these fathers were upper white-collar
professionals and managers. Slightly less than a
fifth were farmers or farm laborers. The remaining 6 out of 10 fathers were blue-collar workers.

The most interesting fact is that occupational changes for fathers of students did not
parallel occupational changes in the total
Southern Negro labor force. There are far lower
proportions of farmers in the labor force in the
mid-1960's than in 1930; white-collar workers have
considerably increased. We may infer, then, that
more Negroes from lower socio-economic families--
blue-collar and farm families--attended college in
1965 than in 1930. However, it is certainly true
that very large proportions of Negro college students, in 1965 as well as in 1930, came from upper
socio-economic families.

CONCLUSIONS

The broad conclusion we reach is that the
Southern primarily Negro college, in terms of its
students, is a remarkably stable institution, and
the majority of the larger of these colleges have
had a lengthy existence.

If one may judge from the press, periodicals,
and other literature, there has been increasing
concern over Southern Negro colleges and their
student enrollments. The colleges themselves have
expressed great interest in expansion, development,

and improvement. This interest has taken many
directions—improvement in the quality of teaching,
expansion of the physical plant, broadening of the
educational offering, de-emphasis of teacher
training curricula—and also recruitment of students from other parts of the country, white students, larger numbers of students with varied
occupational goals, and abler but socio-economi-
cally deprived students.[5]

With regard to the students attending these
colleges, past and present, there seems to have
been little significant change, in spite of wars,
recessions, and changes in educational policies
and legislation. It would seem that the factors
that have induced the same type of Southern Negro
students to enter the Negro colleges are very enduring ones, and that it would require extensive
and well-considered efforts to effect significant
changes in this population. On the other hand, if
it is felt that these colleges are enrolling the
appropriate groups of students, there would appear
to be no problem in continuing to enroll them.

NOTES TO CHAPTER 2

1. In Appendix B is presented a fuller description of the data and the methodology. The
most recent available data are from the 1960 Population Census, thus preventing us from bringing
the historical series up to date. Post-1960
sample survey data collected by the U.S. Bureau
of the Census are not strictly comparable with
the 1960 census data. See U.S. Bureau of the
Census, "Educational Attainment: March 1966 and
1965," Current Population Reports ("Population
Characteristics," Series P-20, No. 158, December
19, 1966), p. 4.

See also A. J. Jaffe and Walter Adams, "Trends in College Enrollment," College Board Review, Winter, 1964-65, No. 55, pp. 27ff.

2. Estimated from data in "Educational Attainment: March 1966 and 1965," op. cit., Tables 1 and 4.

3. Data on enrollment in all Negro colleges, as currently reported by the Office of Education, began about 1940. The statistics of the Office derive from its Biennial Survey of Education in the United States, conducted in even-numbered years, and evidence the same general trend as that of the sample of colleges on which we report here.

4. Ambrose Caliver, A Background Study of Negro College Students, Bulletin No. 8, Office of Education (Washington, D.C.: U.S. Government Printing Office, 1933).

General Studies of Colleges for Negroes, National Survey of the Higher Education of Negroes, Misc. No. 6, Vol. II, Office of Education (Washington, D.C.: U.S. Government Printing Office, 1942).

5. See especially "Negro Higher Institutions in the South" in the Southern Regional Education Board's publication, Regional Action, Vol. 17, No. 2, June, 1966. This article outlines an extensive investigation into the status and problems of Southern primarily Negro colleges, to be undertaken by the Board's recently created Commission on Higher Educational Opportunity in the South. Prominent among the problems which concern the Commission are the high dropout rate at the Negro colleges, attributed to poor preparation at primary and secondary schools; limited curricula at the colleges; the prevailing emphasis on teacher training; and lack of variety in the types of students enrolled.

CHAPTER **3**   RECRUITMENT
PRACTICES*

*1)   The "poor" colleges are expanding
considerably more rapidly than the "good"
colleges.   This is true for total enrollments, but particularly for new entrants,
arguing that the trend has been acceler-
ating in the recent past, especially at
"poor" colleges in the "deep South."*

*2)   The "poor" colleges are less
selective in terms of admissions criteria.
Scholarship is a less frequent criterion
for admission, and the superior scholar is
less frequently mentioned as a particularly
desired element in the student body.   The
"poor" colleges are the ones most frequently satisfied with the students they
are currently enrolling.*

*3)   The "good" colleges have slightly
more financial aid to offer their students.*

---

*This analysis is limited to the four-year
colleges. The two-year private colleges contain
only about 2 per cent of all students enrolled in
Southern Negro colleges. These two-year colleges
may provide a very special educational service,
but clearly are not important for an understanding
of the growth of Negro college enrollment.

*They are somewhat more expensive colleges,
however. Also, whatever the type or quality
of college, availability of Federal student
funds is nearly universal. A considerably
larger proportion of the students at "poor"
colleges have Federal student loans than is
the case for "fair" or "good" colleges.
Apparently the advent of the Federal student
loan and work-study programs, which made
available funds to all qualities and types
of colleges, is an important factor in the
more rapid growth of the "poor" colleges.*

APPLICANTS, ADMISSIONS, AND ENROLLMENTS

About 3 in 10 of all students attending primarily Negro four-year colleges were enrolled in
"good" ones, over 4 in 10 in "fair" ones, and one
fourth in "poor" schools, in 1965 (Chart 3.1).
An essential point of this chapter is that the
present distribution is temporary, and will change
in future years as the numbers of applicants and
new entries to the different quality schools
change. The colleges themselves may change in
quality in the future, thereby altering the distribution of the students, but discussion of such
possible changes is outside the scope of this
volume.

Applicants

The number of applicants rose more than twice
as much in the "deep South"* as in other parts of

---

*The states comprising the "deep South" are:
Alabama, Arkansas, Georgia, Mississippi, and South
Carolina. "Other South" includes: Florida,
Louisiana, North Carolina, Tennessee, Texas, and
Virginia. The border states are: Delaware,

Chart 3.1

Distribution of Students Enrolled in
Four-Year Primarily Negro Colleges,
1965, by Quality of College

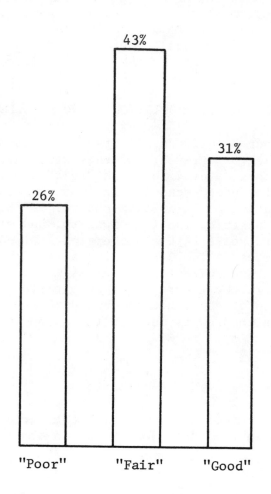

Quality of college

the South. Applicants to "good" colleges actually
decreased a few percentage points in the "deep
South," and rose only modestly, or a little over a
fifth, outside the "deep South." Applicants to
"poor" colleges, whatever the geographical locale,
increased by a half or more, and applicants to
"fair" colleges in the "deep South" rose nearly
this much. The poorer colleges, especially in the
"deep South," apparently are chosen by increasing
proportions of the college applicants.

	Total	Poor colleges	Fair colleges	Good colleges
	%	%	%	%
Deep South	+34	+55	+47	-3
Other South and border states	+15	+49	+2	+22

Acceptance and Entry

The "poor" and the "fair" colleges, as we can
see from the applicant-acceptance rate, became
somewhat more selective between 1962 and 1965 than
the "good" colleges, which have not changed in
this regard (Appendix A, Table 3). All qualities
of colleges have experienced slight increases in
the proportion of accepted students actually enrolling. But the important point is that the
"poor" colleges have experienced larger increases
in applicants than entrants, whereas for the

District of Columbia, Kentucky, Maryland,
Missouri, Oklahoma, and West Virginia.

"fair" and "good" colleges the reverse is true. Apparently the "poor" colleges have experienced the greatest growth in new entrants as a result of very great growth in new applicants, and *in spite of* a somewhat more selective admission policy. The "good" colleges, on the other hand, have experienced less than a third of the growth in applicants that has accrued to the "poor" colleges, and have become *no more selective* regarding admissions.

Finally, we note that in 1965 the differences in the applicant-acceptance rates for the different college groups were insignificant (Appendix A, Table 3). There was, however, a tendency for larger proportions of those accepted by "poor" colleges to actually enter than was the case for "fair" and "good" colleges. Probably more students, when enrollment time actually arrives (Chart 3.2), find themselves only able to afford less expensive colleges, as follows:

	Total	Poor colleges	Fair colleges	Good colleges
% Increase in new entrants, 1962-65	25	43	20	18

Changes in Enrollment

1962-1965

"Poor" and "fair" Negro colleges all increased their *enrollments* by about the same amount between 1962 and 1965, roughly a quarter of the 1962 figure, whereas "good" colleges in-

Chart 3.2

Per Cent Increase in New Entrants to Four-Year Primarily Negro Colleges, 1962-1965, by Quality of College and Location of College

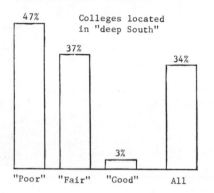

Colleges located in "deep South"

47% "Poor" 37% "Fair" 3% "Good" 34% All

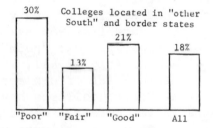

Colleges located in "other South" and border states

30% "Poor" 13% "Fair" 21% "Good" 18% All

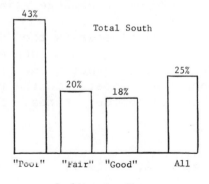

Total South

43% "Poor" 20% "Fair" 18% "Good" 25% All

Quality of college

creased their enrollment by only a sixth. On the
other hand, "poor" colleges increased their *new
entrants* by very nearly a half in the three years,
and "fair" and "good" colleges increased them by
only about a fifth, as follows:*

	Poor colleges	Fair colleges	Good colleges
	%	%	%
Increase in enrollment, 1962–1965	+27	+27	+16
Increase in new entrants, 1962–1965	+43	+20	+18

We know that the increase for "fair" colleges
would have been slightly greater if a student
housing shortage had not forced one very large
"fair" college to reduce its 1965 new entrants.
It is very clear, however, that "good" colleges
are expanding least rapidly of all, whether the
measure be total enrollment or new entrants. It
is also clear that "poor" colleges have increased
their new entrants far more rapidly than all
other qualities or types of colleges, and the
number of new entrants is the measure most sensitive to recent changes in college going.

"Poor" colleges cluster in the "deep South."
Half of the "poor" colleges are located in five
states, and the rest (excepting one "poor" school
not in the South) are located in the twelve remaining Southern and border states. Not

---

*See also Appendix A, Table 1.

unexpectedly, new entrants have increased most
rapidly in the "deep South," where new entrants
to "poor" colleges are a large proportion of all
new entrants (Appendix A, Table 2). Not all the
colleges in the "deep South" are "poor" ones, of
course, and the increase in new entrants for this
sub-region is somewhat less than for the total of
the "poor" colleges. (There are only five "good"
colleges in the "deep South," two of which have
experienced declines in new entrants, 1962-1965.)

The question occurs whether it is characteristics of the "poor" colleges per se, or characteristics of students in sub-regions of the South,
or both of these at once, that are responsible
for the rapid expansion of the "poor" colleges.
The evidence indicates that wherever the "poor"
colleges are located, they are expanding more
rapidly than the "good" colleges, but this is
especially the case in the "deep South." On the
other hand, the "good" colleges in the "deep
South" have hardly expanded at all, whereas those
not in the "deep South" have expanded considerably (though less than "poor" colleges in the
same locale). In addition, the "fair" colleges
in the "deep South" have expanded far more than
those in this quality group located elsewhere.

We assume that the slower growth of the
"good" colleges is in part a matter of more
selective admissions policies. But it also seems
reasonable that it is the characteristics of
students in the "deep South"--lack of funds for
more expensive colleges, lack of adequate primary
and secondary training--that help to account for
the difference in rate of growth in the two sub-
regions of the South. There is the additional
fact that about 1 in 6 of the college entrants
from the "deep South" enter college elsewhere,
and these tend to be the better high school students (Chapter 4). Hardly any college entrants
from "other South," however, select a college in
the "deep South." Apparently this represents

some loss of qualified candidates for the few
"good" colleges in the "deep South."

Estimated 1968 Enrollment

For total enrollments we not only asked for
figures for 1962 and 1965, but also estimates for
1968.* In general, all the colleges expect expansion between 1965 and 1968--expansion of about
a quarter in total enrollment, or about the same
figure as for the actual increase between 1962
and 1965 (Appendix A, Table 1). Whether public
or private, "poor" colleges expect the greatest
expansion of all the four-year colleges, "fair"
colleges the next greatest, and "good" colleges
the least. This accords with the 1962-1965 data
on new entrants which we have just discussed.

RECRUITMENT OF STUDENTS

Almost every college had some sort of an
organized recruitment program. Over 8 out of 10
colleges reported that they have on their staffs
an individual who devotes all, or an important
part, of his time to recruitment (Appendix A,
Table 4). Almost all of the schools reported
recruitment visits to high schools, and several
of those not so reporting had alternative devices,
such as visiting days for high school students
or periodic organized meetings with high school
guidance counsellors within the state. Almost
all colleges stated that their recruitment programs predated 1962. Use of alumni as recruiters,

---

*We do not, of course, claim that what
college officials expect will necessarily occur.
We are primarily interested in such expectations
as they might relate to plans for expansion and
extension of recruitment efforts. (Appendix A,
Table 5, shows these expectations.)

and for the church-related colleges use of church
organizations, were frequently mentioned. About
two thirds of the colleges reported expansion or
intensification of their recruitment efforts
between 1962 and 1965, and 4 out of 5 expect expansion or intensification between 1965 and 1968.
Though the differences are not great, more of the
"poor" colleges expect expansion of their programs
(86 per cent), and fewer of the "good" colleges
(72 per cent), with the "fair" falling in the
middle (81 per cent).

The chief reasons given for expanding recruitment were the desire to get superior students, the simple effect of growth in the college-
age population, growth of the college itself, and
the desire to obtain a more balanced or diversified student population. A balanced or diversified enrollment apparently means attracting such
groups as white students, Negro students from
integrated high schools, and students from a
variety of geographical locations (Appendix A,
Table 5).

Academically able students were desired by
over 8 out of 10 of all the schools, but most of
all, as might be expected, by the "good" colleges
(Appendix A, Table 6). A little over half of all
the schools wanted other than Negro students,
students from the state where the college was
located, and students from deprived backgrounds.
Seven other types of students were mentioned by
smaller proportions of the colleges, ranging from
just under half who sought students from other
parts of the country, to about 1 in 6 who wished
students with particular vocational objectives.
In general, the "good" colleges hoped for a
diverse student body as well as academically
superior students. Large proportions of the
"good" colleges mentioned other than Negro students, students from other parts of the country,
students from deprived backgrounds, and students
with particular vocational objectives. On the

other hand, the "poor" colleges expressed interest in local students; they also welcomed athletes.

About one quarter of the colleges said that the groups of students they wished to enroll were as well represented in the student body as they would wish. Significantly more of the "poor" (36 per cent) expressed satisfaction with their students. Among the "fair" and "good" colleges only 12 per cent were satisfied with their present student representation. This is understandable from one point of view, since the "poor" colleges expressed the least interest in a diversified enrollment, presumably difficult to obtain. On the other hand, over 4 out of 5 of these schools expressed interest in academically superior students, which they certainly do not enroll. One can only infer that academic prowess is perceived relative to expectations, rather than in accordance with fixed standards.

CRITERIA FOR STUDENT ADMISSIONS

By far the *single most important criterion* used by the colleges for selecting students is the student's high school record (Appendix A, Table 7). About 6 out of 10 schools listed this as the one most important, whereas the second most frequently mentioned criterion, graduation from an accredited or approved high school, was mentioned by only 1 out of 10 colleges. Less than 1 out of 10 schools specified test-score data. Simple graduation from high school or the mere desire of a student for a college education was mentioned as the most important criterion by some of the "fair" and "poor" institutions, but by none of the "good" schools. On the other hand, the student's high school record was mentioned by almost three quarters of the "good" schools, but by only about half of the "poor" ones.

Though less than 1 in 10 of the colleges
listed test-score data as the *most important criterion* for selection of students, nearly 6 out of
10 said that such data entered into the admission
decision. Almost three quarters of the "good"
schools (72 per cent) use such data, as compared
to just under half of the "poor" colleges (48 per
cent), and close to 7 of 10 of the "fair" colleges
(67 per cent).

At first glance, one might expect that more
of the colleges would use test-score data, and
that more of those using them would consider them
a better measure of student ability than the high
school record, which is subject to possible mis-
interpretation because of varying qualities of
high schools and high school student bodies. An
untalented student might rank at or near the top
in a high school class composed of poor students,
and vice versa. However, as we discovered from
our attempts to get high school test-score data
for our sample of college entrants, many high
schools do not test their students systematically,
others do not keep methodical records, and still
others use obscure tests which are difficult or
impossible to interpret in relation to more
standard ones. The student's high school standing,
however, is methodically kept by virtually all
high schools, and probably represents the best,
because the most complete, measure of ability
available to the colleges.

Quite clearly, however, the better colleges
employ more stringent academic criteria, and
employ them more frequently, than do the poorer
colleges. This accords with their expressed interest in academically good students, and the
fact that their students ranked considerably
higher on tests of academic ability and achievement.

STUDENT FINANCING

Two comparatively recent developments in the financing of higher education probably have materially affected the college-going plans of Southern Negro high school graduates, in general an economically deprived population. The National Defense Student Act of 1958 initiated a liberal student loan program for college students. Almost any college is eligible to participate in this program, and by 1965 all of the four-year colleges in our study had joined the program. The Economic Opportunity Act of 1964 initiated a work-study program which enables students to earn substantial amounts of money while in college. Only three "poor" colleges had not joined this program by 1965.

In general, then, the great majority of the students in these colleges have access to considerable Federal educational money--money which was not available a few years ago. We may assume that the older loan program is known to almost all students, but that the more recent work-study program may not yet be known to some students (as of the time of our study), and especially may not be known to many high school seniors hoping to arrange college financing. About a quarter of the students in the reporting colleges participate in the loan program, whereas less than a fifth of the students are in the more recent work-study program (Appendix A, Table 8). How many students participate in both programs is not known, but it is clear that the two programs together probably assist more students than do college-financed scholarships. In all instances, save that of "good" colleges, higher proportions of students participate in the Federal loan program alone than receive college scholarship aid.

There is apparently almost no overlap between scholarship aid from the colleges and Federal loans.[1] On the other hand, there is an unknown amount of overlap between the Federal loan and work-aid programs; apparently there is no law which prohibits a student from participating in both Federal programs. As a result some, if not all, of the colleges urge the student to accept work-study aid and thus cut down on the indebtedness which he would acquire from a Federal loan.

Given these observations (and the data in Appendix A, Table 8), it is apparent that over half of all the students in Negro colleges receive scholarship aid from one source or another. If there were no overlap whatsoever among the several sources of funds, about two thirds would be receiving financial assistance.

There is reason to believe that a larger proportion of the students in the "poor" colleges receive Federal assistance than do those in "good" or "fair" ones. If we knew the amount of overlap between the two Federal programs, we would know for certain. The administrators in the "poor" colleges report that about one third of the students receive Federal loans, as compared with one fifth in the better institutions. Furthermore, there is not much difference among the three quality groups in the proportions of students under the Federal work-study program. Finally, when the students themselves were queried (see Chapter 6), about 30 per cent of those in the "poor" schools said they were receiving governmental assistance, as compared with 25 per cent of those in the "fair" and "good" colleges.*

The better colleges, which are generally more affluent, can give scholarship moneys to

---

*The interpretation of these figures is further complicated by the possibility that some students who reported that they worked during the academic year were under the Federal work-study program.

more students, but the students at the less affluent "poor" schools, themselves less affluent students, now have recourse to Federal financing, and
apparently have turned to it to supplement the
less ample supply of college-derived funds.

In terms of the dollar amounts of assistance
per scholarship student, college scholarships are
slightly larger in "good" colleges as compared to
"poor" ones, as follows:

	Poor colleges	Fair colleges	Good colleges
	$	$	$
Dollar amount of aid per student enrolled	60	48	98
Dollar amount of aid per student receiving scholarship aid	305	278	348

The dollar assistance per student enrolled is
about two thirds again as large at the "good"
schools. However, there is not much difference
between the "poor" and "good" colleges in the
amount of aid per student receiving a scholarship.
Hence, we conclude that the "poor" colleges give
their moneys to smaller proportions of the students enrolled, but give each of these students
only slightly less than do the "good" colleges.
Even at the "good" colleges, the average scholarship aid per student receiving such aid is only
about $350, whereas the student loan program pro-
vides for $1,000 per year for an undergraduate
participant, and the work-study program allows a
maximum of $500 per year in compensation.[2] Prior
to the two Federal programs, only very modest
college scholarship moneys were available, and

these were more available at "good" colleges,
whose more affluent students probably needed them
least.

Since the "poor" colleges predominate in the
"deep South," we find that 29 per cent of the students in this sub-region receive such aid, as compared with 27 per cent of the students in "other
South," and 15 per cent in the border states.

The swift rise in new entrants, 1962-1965, as
compared to enrollments, coincides with the period
when the two Federal programs were developing, and
the especially swift rise in new entrants to
"poor" colleges argues that entrance is now
possible to these colleges, given Federal assistance, for expanded proportions of less affluent
high school graduates. Given the less stringent
admittance policies of these schools, together
with this new supply of student funds, all important factors seem to favor continued swift expansion of the "poor" schools. In addition, the
"poor" schools, more satisfied with the kinds of
students they are enrolling than the "good" colleges, also are the schools which most frequently
say they plan to expand recruitment of students.

SOME QUESTIONS

These findings raise fundamental questions.
Is it desirable that the poorer colleges expand
more rapidly than the better colleges? Is higher
education at a "poor" college of any great value
to a student, especially when 9 out of 10 of the
students attending them (according to the college
entrant questionnaire) are in the bottom half of
the national test-score distribution? Presumably
such students are ill-prepared for college-level
work.

Do not these students need considerable
remedial training if they are to obtain skills

and knowledge equivalent to those of most college graduates? Is it likely that "poor" colleges, or even "fair" colleges, can offer such remedial training? Since large proportions of the Southern Negro college students intend to leave the South, will an education at a "poor" college prepare them to compete for good jobs elsewhere?

Is a financial assistance program which fails to take into account the quality of the education a student is seeking, a wise program? Should not students be actively "steered" toward better schools, and the better schools given additional incentives to expand their facilities and entrants? It would seem unlikely that the better schools, concerned as they are with better students, will of their own volition expand to accommodate less proficient ones.

Only about half of the better high school graduates--those in the top half of their classes--planned on entering college in Fall, 1965.[3] Clearly there is a large reservoir of the more able students not planning on college. With adequate incentives, they might be attracted to the better colleges which profess to desire them.

Is it good educational policy for enrollment in Negro colleges in the South to increase very rapidly with little regard to the quality of the education they offer? Social and economic changes are occurring which could affect the future working life opportunities of college-educated Negroes. Historically very many of the Negro professionals serviced the Negro community. Negro children in elementary and secondary schools were taught by Negro teachers, Negro patients went to Negro doctors, etc. Negro professional workers were not very much in competition with white professionals who may have received better educations. As a result the Negro professional, especially in the South, was economically rather successful.[4]

This situation may well be changing. With
school desegregation, for example, nonwhite
teachers are thrown into direct competition with
white teachers. The future competitive position
of future nonwhite professionals may be deteri-
orating precisely at a time when increasing
numbers of Negro students are entering poorer
Negro colleges in the South. Indeed, to compete
successfully in the outside world, the nonwhite
professional ought to be even better educated
than is his white competitor.

Is it possible that the presently "poor" and
"fair" colleges may improve the quality of their
instruction within the foreseeable future? A
number of private agencies and foundations in this
country have recently attempted to raise the
quality of teaching in certain of the primarily
Negro colleges. Highly qualified teachers have
been offered inducements to teach at these schools,
and members of the existing faculties have been
afforded opportunities for further training in
special programs organized at prominent colleges
and universities. Some progress has been made in
developing faculty exchange programs between primarily Negro and primarily white colleges.[5]

According to McGrath, the larger portion of
these efforts is devoted to the colleges which are
already "better" colleges. He also points out
that the weaker colleges cluster in the more
economically disadvantaged states--those least
able to support ambitious development and improvement programs. To our knowledge there are no
Federal moneys (as of late 1967) directly allocated to improvement of the "poorer" Negro colleges.

It is our impression that present measures
aimed at improvement are less than adequate.
McGrath emphasizes the need for massive state and
Federal assistance to these colleges, if any

appreciable progress is to be made in a reasonable span of time. He also notes[6] that large numbers of the primarily Negro colleges do not engage in internal research regarding their academic programs and statuses--or else engage in such research informally and intermittently.

We may note that the experts who rated the colleges for academic quality essentially distinguished "fair" from "poor" colleges on the following basis: "Fair" colleges are ones which, though somewhat deficient at the time of the rating, were felt to have the capacity for considerable improvement over the next few years. "Poor" colleges, on the other hand, not only offered inferior schooling, but also were judged to be unlikely candidates for improvement. In short, to the best of our present knowledge, those colleges classified as "poor" in our study are not likely to improve the quality of their educational offerings significantly within the foreseeable future.

NOTES TO CHAPTER 3

1. When the college students were queried as to the source of their financial support, almost all of those who received any scholarship aid reported receiving but one form. These students were not queried separately about the Federal work-study program.

2. Student Assistance Handbook of the Senate Subcommittee on Education of the Committee on Labor and Public Welfare, Document No. 26 of the 89th Congress, 1st Session (Washington, D.C.: U.S. Government Printing Office, May, 1965), pp. 173 and 190.

3. We estimate as follows: 28 per cent of
all the high school graduates expected to enter
college in Fall, 1965; of these three quarters
were in the top half of their classes. Since the
top half contains 50 per cent of all students, it
would seem that as many, if not more, of the
better students did not expect to enter college
as did.

4. In Human Capital, A Theoretical and
Empirical Analysis, with Special Reference to
Education (New York: National Bureau of Economic
Research, 1964), Gary S. Becker has calculated
rates of return on a college versus a high school
education for whites and nonwhites, and for nonwhites in and out of the South. Apparently the
return for nonwhites is moderately less than for
whites when all important factors are considered,
such as cost of education and increment to income.
Also, the return has been higher for nonwhites in
the South compared with those outside the South,
and here the difference is quite substantial. In
at least partial explanation Becker offers the
thesis that employment discrimination is less for
highly educated nonwhites in the South than outside of the South, and points out that nonwhite
college graduates in the South traditionally enter
occupations which serve a large, segregated nonwhite community. More than half have become
lawyers, doctors, welfare workers, nurses, other
professionals--but *especially school teachers* to
the nonwhite community.

5. Chapters 2 and 7 of Earl McGrath's The
Predominantly Negro Colleges and Universities in
Transition (New York: Teachers College, Columbia
University, 1965), describe a number of these
recent attempts to improve the quality of teaching.

6. Ibid., p. 25.

CHAPTER **4** FROM HIGH
SCHOOL SENIOR
TO COLLEGE
FRESHMAN

1)   *In the Spring of 1965[1] 3 in 10 of
the graduates of primarily Negro high schools
in the South planned on entering college in
the Fall of that year. This corresponds
closely to the proportion of nonwhite high
school seniors throughout the United States
(studied in October, 1965) who said that they
definitely planned on going to college in the
following Fall.*

2)   *That a college education is deemed
highly desirable is shown by the fact that
almost all of the mothers of a cross section
of U.S. nonwhite high school seniors were
reported as favoring a college education for
their children.*

3)   *Just over 1 in 5 Southern Negro high
school graduates selected an integrated
college, almost all in the South. Of these,
over half actually chose public two-year
schools, mostly in Florida, Texas, and
Mississippi.*

4)   Some 3 in 10 of the better students (those in the upper half of the test-score distribution) selected integrated colleges. Another 3 in 10 selected "good" Negro colleges.

5)   Perhaps as many of the better students entered poorer colleges as entered the better ones.

6)   The majority of the poorer students were scheduled to enter the "poor" or "fair" Negro colleges, or public junior colleges.

7)   The larger Southern primarily Negro high schools had the largest proportions of better students intending to enter college. About 4 in 10 of the graduates from high schools sending on 100 or more students to college placed in the upper half of the test scores. Only 2 in 10 graduates from schools sending less than 25 persons to college placed in the upper half.

PROPORTION GOING TO COLLEGE

Of the students who graduated from high school in the Spring of 1965, about 3 in 10 intended to enter college in the Fall of that year. It is certain that more than 30 per cent eventually will enroll since many persons delay entry into college for several years. For example, of the total (whites and nonwhites) college freshman class in October, 1959, a full third had graduated from high school more than a year prior to college entry. Indeed, 1 in 8 of the 1959 college freshman class had graduated from high school in 1954 or earlier.[2]

About 3 in 10 of a U.S. cross section of
white as well as nonwhite high school seniors
surveyed in October, 1965, said that they definitely planned on going to college in the following Fall. In addition, another 5 in 10 of the
nonwhite seniors, and 4 in 10 of the white,
thought that they would go, but were less certain.
The majority of both groups were planning on
finishing at least four years of college, and a
fifth or more reported planning to do graduate
study.[3]

When queried as to their mothers' wishes,
9 in 10 of the nonwhite seniors—and 8 in 10 of
the white—reported that their mothers wished them
to go to college. Regardless of the degree of
accuracy of these proportions—an accuracy which
in the last analysis will be measured only by
actual college attendance—they do indicate that
there is a considerable and widespread urge to go
to college. This is the path toward socio-
economic advancement, or so it is believed.

When queried directly on the best way of
getting ahead in life, the majority of both groups
specified "get a college education." Among the
nonwhite high school seniors about two thirds gave
this answer; a little over half of the white high
school seniors chose "get a college education."
The nonwhite who does reach the senior year of
high school clearly has an urge to continue his
education and may be even more motivated for college than is the white high school senior.

And so they apply for college admission.

NEGRO OR INTEGRATED COLLEGE?

About one Southern Negro high school graduate
out of every five who planned on college selected
what may be termed an "integrated" college.

Almost all of the students in this group selected
Southern integrated colleges; only about 3 per
cent planned to go to Northern or Western colleges
(Chart 4.1).

Just under half of those going to an integrated college chose a four-year one; the large
majority were in the South. Over half planned on
a two-year college, almost all in the South. It
is evident that the large enrollment in integrated
colleges is simply a reflection of the availability of two-year public colleges in a few of
the Southern states, all of which have been designated officially as "integrated"[4] and hence are so
treated in our analysis (Appendix A, Table 9).

Of students graduating from high schools in
the "deep South," fewer (16 per cent) planned on
integrated colleges. Of those graduating from
"other" Southern high schools, many more (27 per
cent) hoped to go to integrated colleges; a little
over half of these youth selected two-year colleges, presumably because all except one of the
states which have developed extensive public
junior college systems are located in this sub-
region.

In terms of both Negro and integrated colleges, it appears that 5 in 6 students planned on
four-year colleges and 1 planned on a two-year
school. Whether those who enrolled in two-year
institutions (in the Fall of 1965) subsequently
entered four-year Negro colleges for their junior
and senior years of study, or integrated ones, we
do not know, but the "rate of transfer" would be
of considerable significance. As will be seen in
Chapter 6, part-college has little future occupational advantages for Negroes, as compared to
the clear and marked advantage conferred by the
full four-year college experience.

Chart 4.1

Distribution of All Spring, 1965, Southern
Negro High School Seniors Planning
on Entering Different Types,
Qualities, and Locations of College

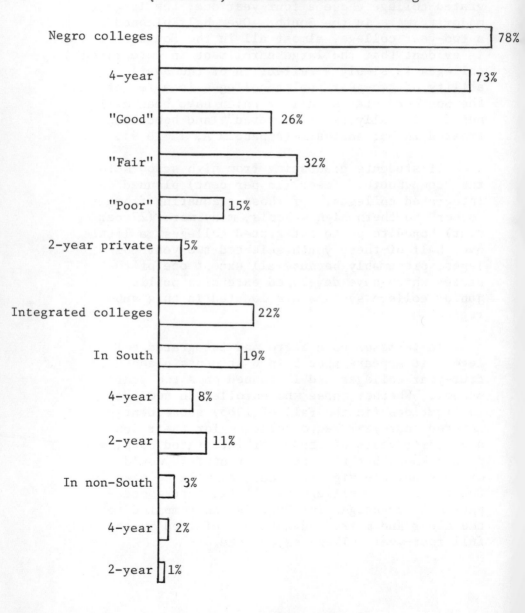

Negro colleges — 78%

4-year — 73%

"Good" — 26%

"Fair" — 32%

"Poor" — 15%

2-year private — 5%

Integrated colleges — 22%

In South — 19%

4-year — 8%

2-year — 11%

In non-South — 3%

4-year — 2%

2-year — 1%

LOCATION OF COLLEGE

Most of the prospective college entrants tended to select a college in the same geographic region as the high school, as follows:

Location of high school	Total	Location of college entered			
		Deep South	Other South	Border states	North and West
Total	100%	38	54	5	3
Deep South	100%	83	11	2	4
Other South	100%	3	87	7	3

Of the approximately 13,000 graduates of high schools in the "deep South" who planned to go to college, an estimated 2,000 were scheduled to enter a college outside of that area, mostly in the "other South." The students who hoped to leave the "deep South" generally were academically abler students; presumably it was chiefly this advantage that enabled them to secure admissions to better colleges located at a distance, and perhaps to secure the student aid necessary to finance this move. The inclination to leave the "deep South" seems reasonable enough, especially for better students, since there are few "good" colleges in the sub-region, and these few are almost all small institutions. As we shall see, better students strongly tended to select better colleges.

Not many students from other areas planned to enter colleges in the "deep South." The total number of students from all other areas who planned to go to a college in the "deep South" was about 2,000,[5] thus equalling the number who left this area.

ACADEMIC RATING OF COLLEGE ENTRANTS
AND TYPE OF COLLEGE ENTERED

Ranking of Students

Slightly over 75 per cent of the Southern
Negro high school graduates entering college in
Fall, 1965, ranked in the top half of their high
school graduating classes, whether the high school
was located in the "deep" or "other South." Test-
score ranking of the entrants, according to
national percentile norms, yielded precisely reverse findings. About 75 per cent of the entrants,
whether from "deep" or "other" Southern high
schools, stood in the bottom half of the national
test-score distribution.* Although the college
entrants from Southern Negro high schools represent, to a marked degree, the abler or more
successful students from these schools, they are
at the same time less able or less well prepared
than students tested throughout the country,
white and nonwhite (Chart 4.2).

The Students With Test-Score Ranking

More of the better students (those who scored
in the top half of the tests) than the poorer ones
tended to plan on the "good" four-year Negro and
the four-year integrated colleges (Chart 4.3).
About 6 in 10 of these better students hoped to
enter these colleges, as compared to about one
third of the poorer students. Many more of the
poorer students were scheduled to enter "fair"

----

*Practically all of the students who ranked
in the top half of the test scores were also in
the top half of their high school graduating
classes.

Chart 4.2

Distribution of Spring, 1965, Southern
Negro High School Seniors Planning on
College by High School and National
Test-Score Standing

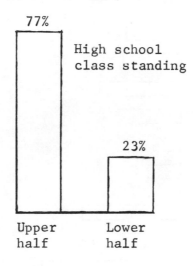

77%

High school
class standing

23%

Upper
half

Lower
half

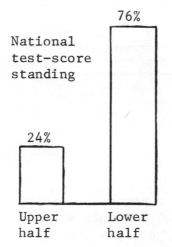

76%

National
test-score
standing

24%

Upper
half

Lower
half

Chart 4.3

Distribution of Southern Negro High School
Seniors, Spring, 1965, Planning on
Entering College, by National Test-Score
Standing and Type of College

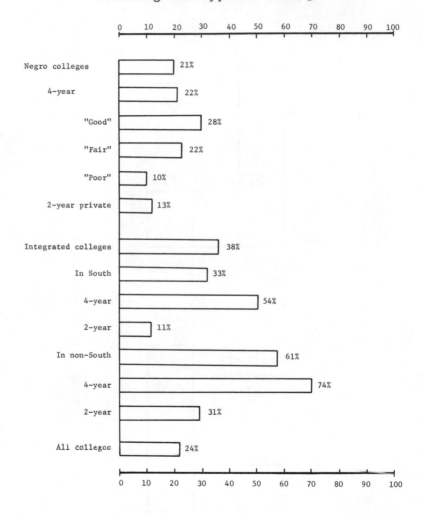

Note: On this chart proportions are based on the
total numbers of students who were tested, and
comparisons may be made with the text table on
page 54 which reports on all students planning
on college, including those who were not tested.

and "poor" four-year Negro colleges and two-year
institutions (Appendix A, Table 10).

Most significantly, some 3 in 10 of the
better students selected integrated colleges,
almost all four-year schools. We do not know
whether these are "good," "fair," or "poor" institutions, and hence cannot evaluate the quality of
the education which they may receive; we only know
that these better students have been lost to the
"good" Negro four-year colleges. Some better
students, of course, may transfer eventually from
integrated to Negro colleges.

Of the poorer students about 16 per cent
chose integrated schools; the majority chose public junior colleges in the South. Where, if any-
where, they will take their junior and senior
studies is not known. However, we hazard a guess
that those who will transfer to four-year colleges
will tend to enter the "fair" or "poor" rather
than the "good" ones.

The drainage was greater out of the "deep"
than "other South." About 3 in 10 of the better
students who graduated from high schools in the
"deep South" planned on integrated four-year
colleges. On the other hand, a little less than
1 in 4 of the better graduates of high schools in
"other South" chose four-year integrated schools.
Presumably the greater availability of "good" primarily Negro colleges in "other South," compared
with "deep South," largely explains this finding.

The Students Without Test-Score Ranking

Some of the high schools either gave no tests,
or gave such obscure ones that they could not be
evaluated.[6] There is reason to think that this
group of schools may be of lower academic quality
than those high schools which gave well-known
tests. We do know that less than 1 in 5 of these

high school graduates planning on college chose a
"good" four-year college. Although almost 30 per
cent chose integrated ones, the majority selected
two-year public colleges in the South.

The Colleges

What calibre of students did the various
types of colleges receive? Our only measure of
"calibre of students" is that of test-score
ranking--upper half, lower half, or no tests
given. This threefold classification suggests
that the four-year colleges outside of the South--
the North and West--received the best students;
57 per cent were in the upper half of the test-
score distribution, 21 per cent were in the lower
half, and only 22 per cent had no test scores.
The integrated four-year colleges in the South
received the next best group of college entrants,
followed by the "good" and then the "fair" Negro
four-year institutions. The "poor" four-year
schools and all the junior colleges (most of
which are integrated) received the least qualified
student body. The data are as follows:

	Southern colleges					North and West, 4-year
	Negro 4-year			Inte-grated 4-year	2-year	
	Good	Fair	Poor			
	%	%	%	%	%	%
Total	100	100	100	100	100	100
Upper half	22	16	7	38	7	57
Lower half	57	56	64	33	49	21
No test scores	21	28	29	29	44	22

Of most significance is the fact that perhaps
only half of the best students (those who ranked
in the upper half of the test scores) planned to
enter the better colleges. We cannot pinpoint
this proportion since we have no information about
the quality of the integrated colleges, or those
outside of the South. We only know that the number of better high school graduates who planned to
go to "fair" and "poor" four-year Negro colleges
was about equal to the number entering "good"
ones. In addition, a significant number of the
better students expected to enter integrated colleges and two-year schools.

LOCATION OF HIGH SCHOOL IN RELATION TO
QUALITY AND TYPE OF COLLEGE ENTERED

The region of the high school from which the
college entrant graduated emerged as a very significant predictor of the quality of college he
hoped to enter. Of the college entrants from
"other South" who planned to attend four-year
Negro colleges, about half selected "good" colleges. Only about a fifth of the entrants from
the "deep South," however, chose "good" colleges.

Since practically no differences were found
by sub-region of high school within the South in
proportions of college entrants ranking high and
low on the two academic indicators (class standing
and test-score rank), it may be asked why the sub-
region yields such large differences in proportions going on to different qualities of college.
Since over 40 per cent of the college entrants
attended high schools in the "deep South," the
question assumes considerable importance.

The answer is simple. Since the academically
better high school graduate from the "deep South"
did not have easy and close access to a "good"
Negro college, he expected to enroll in a "fair"

or "poor" one. The better student from "other
South," however, was in closer proximity to more
"good" Negro colleges, and so chose one. The tendency for the better students to enter better
colleges is quite severely modified by the differ-
ential availability of better colleges in the two
sub-divisions of the South which we studied. Very
few students are able to enter a better college
far from home in preference to a poorer local
school.

SEX DISTRIBUTION OF THE COLLEGE ENTRANTS

Within our sample about 4 in 10 of college
aspirants were males, and 6 in 10 females. The
proportion of women planning to enter college was
lower in the more integrated "other South," and we
assume that this proportion would further decrease
as one moved from "other South" to the border
states, and finally to locales outside the South
entirely.[7]

There is very little difference between males
and females in the tendency to enroll in a local
college. Possibly a few more women tend to select
local colleges, but if so, this difference is of
little consequence to college administrators.

With reference to academic ability, there are
about equal proportions of males and females in
the top and bottom halves of the national test-
score distribution. It would appear that, insofar
as the tests are adequate measures, the two sexes
are about equal in academic aptitude. However,
larger proportions of women than men rank high in
their high school classes; this is true for both
regions of the South. Just under 7 out of 10 of
the men were in the top half of their high school
classes, and between 8 and 9 out of 10 of the
women. We cannot explain this finding, but can
only assume that it stems from complex causes,

differentially motivating the two sexes toward
academic achievement.

CHARACTERISTICS RELATED TO
HIGH SCHOOLS AND COLLEGES

There is a moderate tendency for students who
enter college from high schools with large graduating classes to be better students than those
from high schools with small graduating classes.
This is clearest in "other South" (Appendix A,
Table 11). The graduating classes of high schools
where large numbers of the graduates plan to enter
college are very likely to have large proportions
of academically able students. This is especially
true of the "deep South," where only about 13 per
cent of the entrants from high schools sending
less than twenty-five students on to college
ranked in the top half of the national test-score
distribution. Nearly half of the students from
high schools sending 100 or more students ranked
in the top half. For "other South" the equivalent
proportions were 23 and 27 per cent--a large difference, though a considerably smaller one than
for "deep South" (Appendix A, Table 12). We know
that the larger schools send on the highest proportions of able students, but we do not know
whether this is the result of better teaching in
the larger high schools, a greater emphasis on
college going, or other factors.

The better students from both sub-regions of
the South tend to choose larger colleges, whether
the measure of student quality is test-score rank
or high school class standing (Appendix A, Table
13).

NOTES TO CHAPTER 4

1.   The high school seniors' plans are close approximations of what they probably did regarding college, since the plans were reported by high school guidance personnel and other responsible officials at the schools, rather than by the students.   Specific colleges were named for each student planning on college, presumably representing acceptance of the student by the college.   Some students, of course, not reported as planning on college, might well secure admission at the last moment, and some small proportion of those accepted by colleges might fail to enter.

2.   See U.S. Bureau of the Census, "Educational Status, College Plans, and Occupational Status of Farm and Nonfarm Youths: October 1959," Farm Population (Series Census-ERS [P-27], No. 30, August, 1961), Table 3.

3.   Preliminary unpublished findings from a Bureau of Applied Social Research study currently in progress and supported by the U.S. Office of Education.   The data were collected by the U.S. Bureau of the Census as part of the Current Population Survey.

4.   See also Appendix B, "Methodology," Part III.

5.   Estimated on the basis of location of high school for students enrolled in Negro colleges in the "deep South."

6.   See Appendix B, "Methodology," Part II.

7.   The 1964 Office of Education figures from the Statistical Abstract, for entrants to all primarily Negro colleges, record slightly larger proportions of boys than is the case for our sample.

Students included in the Office of Education tabulations attended high school in all parts of the
country, however, whereas our high school graduates attended high school in the Southern states
exclusively. For the country as a whole,
according to the 1960 Census, Negro men and women
enter college with about equal frequency. In
other words, outside the South Negro men are somewhat more likely to enter college than are women.
Had the Office of Education tabulations excluded
graduates from non-Southern and border high
schools, we believe that the two sets of figures
on the sex distribution of college entrants would
have been very nearly identical.

CHAPTER **5** THE
COLLEGE
STUDENTS

1)   *The students who attend primarily*
Negro colleges generally come from higher
socio-economic backgrounds, when compared
with all Southern Negro families. The
better the quality of the college attended,
the higher the socio-economic status.

2)   *The great majority of students*
graduate from high schools in the same
state as the college they enter, but the
better the college the larger the propor-
tion who travel a considerable distance to
attend it.

3)   *Though most students attended*
high school in the South, fully two thirds
intend to leave the South following the
completion of their education. Existing
data on recent out-migration appear to
indicate that perhaps half of this group
will migrate, though not immediately
following graduation.

4)   *Education is the major subject*
most frequently selected, and teaching is
the occupation students most frequently
expect to enter, whatever the quality of

60

*college. Larger proportions of students
in "poorer" colleges than in "better" ones,
however, are educational majors, and larger
proportions hope to teach.*

*5) Financial help from families is
the most frequently mentioned source of
college funds; this is most often the case
for students at "better" colleges, who
come from somewhat more affluent families.*

*6) Government financial assistance,
available at almost all the colleges regardless of quality, is cited by about a
quarter of the students. Apparently more
of the students in "poor" colleges receive
such assistance.*

SOCIAL AND ECONOMIC BACKGROUND

These students tend to come from families in
the higher socio-economic brackets; their parents
had more schooling, and many more of them were in
white-collar jobs, in comparison with the Southern
Negro population. The students in the two
Northern Negro institutions had the highest social
and economic background, followed by those in
four-year private Negro colleges and those
attending integrated institutions in the South.
Students in the four-year public accredited colleges were somewhat lower, and those in nonaccredited four-year schools lower yet. Those
attending two-year schools were almost identical
with the general Negro population of the South in
regard to family income and parents' education and
occupations.

The "good" colleges had the students with the
highest social and economic background. Median
family income was $5,300 in the "good," $4,100 in
the "fair," and $3,300 in the "poor" colleges. In

the nonaccredited schools it was $3,200, in the
two-year colleges $2,700, and among all Negro
Southern families $2,900 (Appendix A, Tables 14
to 19 inclusive).

REGION OF ORIGIN AND FUTURE HOPES

More of the students in the "good" colleges
and those in the Northern Negro institutions tend
to come from out of state, whether measured in
terms of state of birth or of high school graduation (Chart 5.1). Since their families are
better off financially, they can afford to go
to these better schools, wherever they may be
located. Students in the "poor" accredited and
the nonaccredited and two-year schools are almost
all of local origin; this probably reflects, in
part at least, the economic factor. The students
at integrated schools also tended to be almost
entirely of local origin.[1]

An estimated 7 in 10 of all students
attending four-year colleges in the South graduated from a local high school--one in the same
state as the college. Of those who crossed a
state line to enter college, over half went to
a "good" college.

When asked where they wanted to live after
finishing their education, somewhat less than 1
in 3 chose the South. There was not much difference by type of college (Appendix A, Tables 20 to
23 inclusive). These expectations to leave the
South are very likely to come true for many (see
Chapter 6).

SCHOLASTIC CHARACTERISTICS

There is very little difference by type or
quality of school for:

Chart 5.1

Distribution of Students by Quality of College, 1965, and by Location of High School and of College

High school and college
in same Southern state

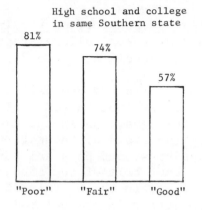

High school and college in
same Southern region, but
in different states

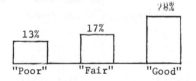

High school not in the
South, college in the
South

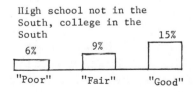

Quality of college

1. <u>Degree credit</u>. Almost 9 in 10 report studying for a degree. The proportion was only slightly less in the two-year colleges.

2. <u>Full-time students</u>. Nearly all report being full-time students.

3. <u>College preparatory curriculum</u>. Over 3 in 4 report having taken college preparatory work in high school (Appendix A, Table 24).

Between one third and one half of the students in the "poorer" accredited colleges, in the nonaccredited colleges, and in the two-year colleges reported the field of "education" (including elementary, business, and physical education) as their major. About half of the students in the "good" colleges and in the Northern Negro institutions were majoring in the natural and social sciences. Less than one quarter chose the field of education. As will be seen, these fields of study are related to choice of occupation; far more of the students from the "poor" colleges expect to be teachers.[2]

Just over 22 per cent of all 1964 bachelor's and first professional degree recipients,[3] white and nonwhite, majored in education. We do not have the data for white graduates alone, but since Negro graduates were a small percentage of the total, the proportion for both color groups would approximate that for white students. When we compare this national figure of 22 per cent with the proportion of education majors at the various types and qualities of primarily Negro colleges (Appendix A, Table 23), we find that the proportions majoring in education at private accredited and "good" Negro colleges are almost identical with the 1964 national figure just cited. The proportion at the two Northern colleges is slightly lower than the national figure. At all

other types and qualities of colleges the proportion is considerably higher, and is highest of all
at the "poor" colleges (47 per cent), or more than
twice the national proportion.

OCCUPATIONAL PLANS

Over 3 in 4 of all students report that they
plan to go on to graduate or professional school,
regardless of differences in type or quality of
school. These expectations appear to be unrealistic since the proportion of all U.S. college
graduates who go on to postgraduate college
training is considerably less than 3 in 4. On
the other hand, perhaps all those who expect to
become teachers realistically plan to study at
teachers' colleges, if not immediately, at some
point in their academic careers. For further discussion of this question see Chapter 6 (Appendix
A, Table 24).

Virtually all the students expect to enter
white-collar occupations (Chart 5.2). This is to
be expected, since there is little point in going
to college to prepare for manual work. Within
the white-collar category almost all specify a
professional or technical job.

Of the students enrolled in "good" colleges
and the Northern Negro colleges, about one third
hope to become teachers, but only a small fraction
aspire to be college teachers. At the "poor"
colleges, including the nonaccredited ones and
two-year institutions, some 2 students in 3 expect
to become teachers. Among the students in "fair"
colleges, and those attending integrated colleges,
5 in 10 hope to teach.

About half of all the students report
teaching as their expected occupation. This percentage is much higher than that among all college

Chart 5.2

Distribution of Students by Quality of College, 1965, and Occupational Choice

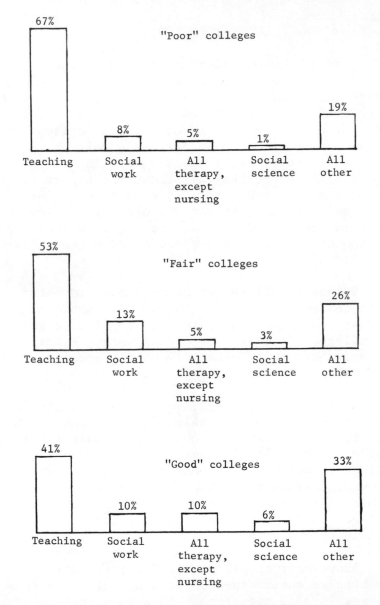

Occupational preference

students in the United States. It probably reflects the fact that a large fraction of the students in Negro colleges in the South are women,
and that teaching is a traditional occupation for
the Southern Negro woman. It certainly reflects
an awareness of the historical opportunity in the
South for college-educated Negroes to secure
employment as instructors to the segregated school
population of Negro children. We do not know
whether this historical awareness on the part of
the college students may obscure for them the
increasing white-collar opportunities in other
occupations. This question is discussed at
greater length in Chapter 6.

If all these students should realize their
expectations as regards teaching, we can be sure
that few of the future teachers will have graduated from "good" colleges. Of those who may
become teachers in the late 1960's, we estimate
that:*

    22 per cent will be graduates of "good"
       colleges,
    47 per cent of "fair" colleges, and
    31 per cent of "poor" schools (in
       cluding nonaccredited).

We noted previously that the poorer schools
apparently are increasing their enrollment more

---

*This calculation is based on the estimated
enrollment in "good," "fair," and "poor" primarily
Negro colleges, derived from statistics supplied
by college officials for our "recruitment questionnaire." Proportions of students hoping to
teach at the three quality groups of colleges
derive from responses to the survey of students
attending primarily Negro colleges.

rapidly than the better schools. If this continues, after 1970 an even larger proportion of
the teachers will be graduates of the poorer colleges (Appendix A, Tables 25 and 26).

HIGH SCHOOL STANDING

At the "good" four-year accredited colleges,
70 per cent of the students reported that they had
been in the upper quarter of their high school
graduating classes. On the other hand, these good
students accounted for 46 per cent of those
attending four-year nonaccredited schools, and
only 30 per cent of those at two-year schools. We
believe that the differences in high school scholastic achievement are even greater than these
percentages indicate because the students in the
better colleges probably came from better high
schools. Hence, a graduate from an inferior high
school could be in the top quarter of his graduation class and still be more poorly equipped,
academically, than a student who was in the second
quarter of the graduation class at a superior high
school (Appendix A, Table 27).

FINANCING OF COLLEGE

Somewhat under half of the Negro college students obtain their financial support from one
source only; the others report two, three, or more
sources of funds. The single most important
source is the student's immediate family. A somewhat larger proportion of those going to four-year
private accredited schools report this than of
those enrolled in nonaccredited or two-year
schools. The slight difference is in agreement
with the findings on family income; those
attending four-year private colleges come from
wealthier families.

Federal government aid in the form of loans and work-study programs is quite significant in helping the student finance his college education. About 30 per cent of those in "poor" colleges (including the nonaccredited schools) reported that they were receiving "government loan or other government aid," as compared with a quarter of the students in "fair" and "good" schools. Included in "government aid" is an unknown, but probably relatively small amount of non-Federal money. It is possible that there is also some overlap between "other government aid" and "work during school year"; this latter could include the Federal work-study program.

These Federal loans and aids are given to the student, apparently with no consideration of the quality of the school which he attends. Whether this procedure will result in the educational equivalent of Gresham's law is a moot point. If financing is equally available for schools of all qualities, will the "bad drive out the good?" (Appendix A, Table 28).

PERSONAL CHARACTERISTICS

There is little difference among the several types and qualities of colleges regarding such characteristics as age, sex, marital status, year in college, residence while attending college, and person who encouraged student to attend college (Appendix A, Tables 29 to 31 inclusive).

NOTES TO CHAPTER 5

1. Our information about students attending integrated four-year Southern colleges is limited to three public institutions in Oklahoma, Louisiana, and Texas. Accordingly, these data

may not reflect the situation for all integrated four-year colleges throughout the South.

2. Our classification of the major subject reported by the students follows the criteria of the Office of Education. Because our data are comparable with those of the Office of Education, we considerably understated the proportions of students in teacher preparatory courses of study. The Office's classification is by major area of specialization. For example, majors in English education or history education are classified under English or history, since the larger part of the course work is generally concerned with English or history, rather than with the teaching of these subjects per se. Majors in elementary or secondary education, of course, are classified as education majors. Majors in specialized educational fields, such as physical education or music education, are also classified as education majors, on the premise that in such instances the teaching itself is especially prominent. Very probably this mode of classification, the one in general use, explains in part the considerably greater proportions of students in our study planning to teach than majoring in education.

3. <u>Summary Report on Bachelor's and Higher Degrees Conferred During the Year 1963-64</u>, U.S. Office of Education, Department of Health, Education, and Welfare, Circular OE-54010-64.

CHAPTER ASPIRATIONS
AND
REALITIES

College students generally aspire to the
probable. If history is any guide to the future,
then large numbers--those who finish four years of
college--will realize their goals to a significant
degree, if not entirely.

*1) A significant number who begin
college will not receive their baccalaureate. Historically, only about half
have graduated.*

*2) Students who do <u>complete four
years of college</u> appear likely to fulfill
their occupational aspirations in the large
majority of instances. Most will become
upper white-collar workers. Most of the
education majors, as well as a considerable
number who did not major in education, will
become teachers. Initially, at least, most
of the teachers will instruct Negro primary
and secondary pupils in the South.*

*3) Students who <u>do not complete four
years of college</u> are far less likely to
realize these occupational goals. Only a
small number of these college dropouts will*

71

become white-collar workers. It is possible
for many Southern white college dropouts to
find employment as white-collar workers, but
such opportunities for Negroes are much more
limited. The white-collar jobs which are
open to nonwhites usually require completion
of college.

4) Relatively few of the large proportion of the 1965 students who plan to
attend graduate or professional school
appear likely to do so--at least in the
immediate post-graduation period. There is
evidence that many will do graduate work
when they are past their mid-twenties, particularly those who will teach. It seems
unlikely, however, that the number of these
graduate students will ever equal the 80 per
cent of 1965 undergraduates who plan on extended schooling.

5) In general, the 1965 students
appear to have based their occupational
aspirations on what appear to them realistic
criteria. While the great majority aspire
to upper white-collar jobs--and this represents a considerable departure from the job
experience of their fathers, most of whom
were blue-collar workers--they still select
those occupations, such as teaching, where
they feel least disadvantaged in comparison
with white persons with equivalent qualifi-
cations for employment. It cannot be said
whether or not the jobs most of the students
hope to get are the only good jobs open to
them, since we are not sure to what extent
opportunities in managerial and clerical and
sales employment have increased for qualified Negroes in recent years.

6) Most of those who go to work
following graduation will work in their

*home states. Small proportions will work
in other Southern states or will leave the
South. As time passes more of them will
leave the South; just how many will depend
on where the employment opportunities will
be. About 7 in 10 of the 1965 students
planned to leave the South, but this
aspiration seems unlikely to be fulfilled
for most graduates.*

BACKGROUNDS AND GOALS

Most of the Negro college students represent
the first generation of their families to attend
college. Depending on the type and quality of
college where the son or daughter was enrolled,
from 1 to 3 in 10 of the students' fathers completed a year or more of college. Not only is
college attendance itself a departure from past
experience in these families, but the students
also have further and even greater departures in
mind.

1) Clearly the first step is to complete four years of college.

2) About 8 in 10 of the students plan
   on attending graduate or professional school, further widening
   the educational gulf between them
   and their parents.

3) Virtually all of the students hope
   to work in professional and technical jobs--the upper white-collar
   occupations. Well over half expect
   to teach. Only about 1 in 4 of
   their fathers were white-collar
   workers, and only about 1 in 5
   upper white-collar workers.

4) Although about 9 in 10 of the
students were born and attended
high school in the Southern or
border states, about 7 in 10 hope
to live in the North or West after
completing their educations.

The total orientation of these students is clearly
toward upward socio-economic mobility. How likely
are they to realize their aspirations?

COMPLETING FOUR YEARS OF COLLEGE

Not all of those who enter college complete
four years of study--their undergraduate work.
In the past, for the total United States, only
between 40 and 50 per cent of the nonwhites who
entered college completed their undergraduate
study.[1]

There is some evidence that among Negro students who attend integrated colleges, a higher
proportion receive their baccalaureate.[2] Clark
and Plotkin report that the Negro dropout rate
in segregated colleges is about equal to that of
white students, but "The dropout rate for these
Negro students who had some type of contact with
the National Scholarship Service and Fund for
Negro Students and attended integrated colleges
is less than one quarter the national average
dropout rate. This suggests that these students
were better selected or were more highly motivated or both."[3]

The authors contrast the Negro students at
integrated colleges with those who attend predominantly Negro colleges.

. . . the decision to enter an inter-
racial college rather than a segregated one probably reflects a tendency
or conscious desire to break through

the existing racial barriers. Thus,
the Negro students in this study not
only are motivated by economic, academic, and status considerations, but
also are reinforced by their attempt to
achieve racial equality through personal goals.

The Negro student in predominantly
Negro colleges, on the other hand,
cannot hope to break through racial
barriers by education alone. This may
account for their adoption of other
methods to achieve racial break-
throughs.[4]

The factors which Clark and Plotkin found to
be associated with success--graduation from an
integrated college--are: better high school
grades and test scores, somewhat higher family
income, father being in a white-collar occupation,
both parents having attended college. Differences in success were also noted according to
major field of study, source of scholarship funds,
type of college attended, and part of the country
in which the high school was located.[5]

What is most pertinent for the students in
the predominantly Negro colleges is that so many
of them, especially in the "poor" and "fair"
colleges, do not have the attributes which are
associated with success. In comparison with those
attending four-year "good" Negro or integrated
colleges, these students have lower test scores,
lower family income, more fathers who were manual
or farm workers, and parents who had less education. Those attending two-year colleges had even
fewer of the attributes leading to success.

The prognosis appears to be, then, that large
numbers of the students, especially those in two-
year colleges and in the "poor" and "fair" four-
year Negro colleges, will not achieve their first

ambition--receipt of a baccalaureate. Very likely
the proportion who are successful will continue to
be of the historical order of 40 to 50 per cent of
those who enter college.

ATTENDING GRADUATE SCHOOL

Over three quarters of the students in the
Negro colleges stated that they planned to attend
graduate or professional school. This appears to
be unrealistic and is contrary to the available
historical data. The expectations of the women
seniors seem possible, but those of the men seem
exaggerated in light of past history. In 1960
the proportion of all Negroes who had a baccalaureate and had gone on to graduate work was as
follows:[6]

Age	Males	Females	Period of high school graduation
25-29	40	24	early 1950's
30-34	48	32	late 1940's
35-44	51	38	around 1940
45-54	51	38	around 1930

Among Negroes living in the South in 1960
somewhat smaller proportions had done graduate
study.

Another indication that the hopes of these
students are not likely to be realized comes from
a survey taken in the Fall of 1965 of a cross
section of all nonwhite high school seniors in the
United States. Two thirds of the males and one
third of the females said that they planned on

graduate school.[7] These students represented
only about half of the entire group.

Apparently many of the Negro college graduates undertake their graduate or professional
school work some years after completing the four
years of undergraduate study rather than entering
graduate school immediately after receiving their
first degree. By about age thirty-five most who
ever undertake graduate study have done so.

One study which followed up graduates from
four Negro four-year colleges in Louisiana[8] shows
that either there is a considerable time lag
between college graduation and post-graduate
study, or that comparatively few who plan on it
do in fact enter graduate school. A sample of
1964 graduates was surveyed about one and a half
years later, in the fall of 1965. Over 9 in 10
of these students had said that they planned on
advanced study *eventually*. However, 2 in 5 of
the men, and 1 in 4 of the women, said they
planned on graduate study *immediately* following
the baccalaureate. Actually, in the year and a
half following graduation only 1 in 5 of the men,
and 1 in 16 of the women, had entered graduate
school. Undoubtedly many more will eventually do
graduate study, but it seems very unlikely that
9 in 10 will do so.

OCCUPATIONAL CHOICE

The Students' Beliefs

The Negro college students themselves believe
that they are being realistic about their occupational goals. A recent survey asked the students
in primarily Negro colleges to rate various occupational categories by the extent of "social
difficulty" they would anticipate if they
attempted to enter them.[9] "Social difficulty"
represents the student's estimate of his chance

of obtaining employment in a particular type of
job when competing for it with an equally qualified white applicant. Not unexpectedly, farm jobs
and blue-collar jobs were perceived by the students as being the least "socially difficult"
types of jobs, though hardly any of the students
wished to enter such occupations. Regarding the
white-collar occupations for which college ostensibly prepares students, and which Negro students
did hope to enter, we note:

Occupation	Michigan study: extent of social difficulty	Our study: popularity of occupation
Teaching	Least difficulty	Greatest popularity
All other professional and technical	Next to least difficulty	Next to greatest popularity
Clerical and sales	Next to greatest difficulty	Next to least popularity
Managers, officials, and proprietors, except farm	Greatest difficulty	Least popularity

It is a moot point whether or not the Negro
students are correct in their assessment of the
current "social difficulty" of the various occupational categories. There is evidence that government hiring and "equal opportunity" policies and
legislation have reduced somewhat the incidence of
racial discrimination in employment.[10] On the
other hand, such changes may not have been large

and visible enough to alter the students' estimates, presumably based on relative opportunity in
the past.

The important point is that the students profess to occupational goals which accord with
opportunity *as they perceive it,* and in all
probability will attempt to enter precisely the
occupations they *believe* are most accessible,
whether or not they are in fact correct in these
beliefs.

The College Graduates

Most of the nonwhite men--about 9 in 10 in
the total United States--who had completed five
or more years of college study were in white-
collar jobs in 1960, and most of these were professional and technical workers. Among those who
had finished only four years of college, about
three quarters were in white-collar jobs, but only
half were professional and technical workers.
There is a question, of course, as to which comes
first, graduate school study or the professional
job. In view of the fact that so many nonwhites
do graduate study some years after completing the
baccalaureate, it would appear that initial entry
into a professional or technical job often leads
to entering a graduate school, and therefore the
person will continue working in a professional
occupation. Some men, of course, who plan to
enter such fields as medicine or law, will enter
a graduate or professional school immediately
after receiving the baccalaureate; for them graduate study must precede professional employment
(Appendix A, Table 33).

Rather few nonwhite college graduates--per-
haps only 1 in 8--become blue-collar workers or
farmers. If the man has completed one or more
years of graduate study, he is almost certain not
to be in these lower status jobs. However, of

those having completed only four years of college, one fifth find employment in blue-collar or agricultural jobs.

In comparison with white men, the nonwhite college graduate differs in two respects. More nonwhites are elementary and secondary school teachers, whether they have had only four years of college or have had graduate study (Appendix A, Table 34). Furthermore, more nonwhite than white college graduates are employed in blue-collar jobs. The difference is particularly great for those who have only the baccalaureate.

We may consider that the employment experiences (in 1960) of nonwhite men in the South, aged thirty to thirty-four, are the best indicator of the short-run possibilities open to the 1965 Negro college students if and when they graduate. (Comparison of this group with total U.S. nonwhites, aged twenty-five and over, reveals very similar patterns.) Whether the Negro college male graduates remain in the South or whether they migrate to the North and West as so many plan to do, they are likely to find themselves in substantially similar types of occupations.

Among women college graduates, both the whites and nonwhites are largely professional and technical workers. Teachers predominate in both groups. As among men, larger proportions of the nonwhite than of the white women are elementary and secondary school teachers; this is true both for those having four years of college and those with graduate study. More white than nonwhite women college graduates are in lower white-collar jobs, and fewer are in blue-collar jobs. As was observed with the nonwhite male college graduates, employment opportunities for the women are substantially the same whether they remain in the South or migrate out.

The College Dropouts

The nonwhite male student who fails to obtain his baccalaureate is more likely to be a blue- than a white-collar worker. He has very little chance of entering a professional or technical job except at a semi-professional level.[11] Indeed, the white man with only a high school education is likely to have about as good a job as does the nonwhite with only one to three years of college work (Appendix A, Table 33). Either the nonwhite makes it or he fails. Completion of four years of college may mean an upper white-collar job. Failure to complete college will mean job failure for many, since virtually all of the students aspire to upper white-collar jobs.

More nonwhite women than men who are college dropouts may expect to get white-collar jobs. Among the women, close to 6 in 10 had such jobs in 1960, although the majority were lower white-collar. The white woman college dropout is much more likely than the nonwhite to be in a white-collar job, albeit lower white-collar (clerical and sales jobs).

Despite the fact that the nonwhite college dropout does not have as high status a job as the white dropout, he is likely to have a better job than his former nonwhite schoolmates who only completed high school. Among the high school graduates, some 2 or 3 in 10--both men and women--had white-collar jobs. Among those with one to three years of college, about 4 in 10 had white-collar jobs.

Teaching

Teaching in elementary and secondary schools is the most frequent job for professional Negroes, especially in the South. The proportions of all

professional workers who were teachers in 1960
were as follows:

	Men	Women
Total U.S.		
White	9%	43%
Nonwhite	27%	57%
South		
White	10%	46%
Nonwhite	44%	74%

Most of the nonwhite teachers--9 in 10 of the
men, and over 8 in 10 of the women--are college
graduates. Furthermore, about half of the nonwhite men have done graduate study in 1960, and
about one third of the women.[12]

	Per cent finishing four years or more of college	
	Men	Women
Total	87	83
Under 35 years of age	87	83
35 to 44 years	91	87
45 and over	85	78

| | Per cent finishing one or more years of graduate study | |
	Men	Women
Total	41	27
Under 35 years of age	28	19
35 to 44 years	54	35
45 and over	54	25

At ages under thirty-five somewhat fewer of both groups have gone on to graduate study, but by about age thirty-five most of those who will have entered graduate school have done so. Of the older nonwhite men over half have completed one or more years of graduate study.

The follow-up study of the Louisiana college students[13] reveals that a large proportion of this group became teachers upon receiving their baccalaureate. Of those who had been education majors in college, between 8 and 9 in every 10 took teaching jobs as their initial employment. In addition, nearly 1 in 5 who had not majored in education entered teaching. Altogether, 69 per cent of the graduates who obtained employment were teachers.

The Louisiana study also affords some insight into the academic characteristics of the Negro teachers in Fall, 1965, and of the types of pupils they taught. Students of low ability, as measured by their college records, were considerably more likely to enter teaching than those of high ability, and they were considerably less likely to enter other occupations. This was more clearly the case for the men. Among both men and

women, well over 9 out of 10 taught Negro pupils
exclusively.

It is clear that the aspiration of so many
of the college students to become teachers is
likely to be realized. Indeed, for Negro women
who remain in the South there appears to be little
alternative; teaching is the most readily available professional job. But in order to be
teachers they must be college graduates, so there
is a built-in college-occupational-graduate study
pattern. To forge ahead in the teaching pro-
fession, especially in those school districts
which peg pay levels to number of years of graduate study completed, they must attend graduate
school. The Negro college students undoubtedly
understand this pattern.

WILL THEY LEAVE THE SOUTH?

At the most, probably only half of the 7 in
10 students who said that they planned to migrate
out of the South after graduation will do so.
Historically, migration out of the South has
fluctuated in accordance with job opportunities.
An indication of how employment opportunities for
Negro college graduates vary from region to region
and time to time is seen by noting the change in
numbers of Negro employed professionals:

	South	North and West
Between 1940 and 1950		
Increase in number of:		
male professional workers	10,200	7,300
female professional workers	21,400	16,000
Total	31,600	23,300

	South	North and West
Between 1950 and 1960		
Increase in number of:		
male professional workers	12,800	24,300
female professional workers	31,000	39,600
Total	43,800	63,900

In the decade 1940 to 1950, the absolute number of professional jobs increased significantly more in the South than in the rest of the country. Presumably there was comparatively less job incentive for migration. Between 1950 and 1960, however, the number of professional jobs increased more in the North and West than in the South.

Some indication of the extent of migration out of the South is given by the fact that about one third of the Southern born Negro men who had finished four years or more of college had left the South by 1960.[14] When they migrated, or where they received their college education, is unknown. Nevertheless, this proportion--one third--is less than half of the proportion of 1965 college students who said that they planned on leaving the South.

Perhaps out-migration from the South was greater in the latter half of the 1950's than at other times. About one fifth of the men and one sixth of the women aged twenty-five to twenty-nine in 1960, and who were college graduates, left the South between 1955 and 1960. With increasing age proportions were much smaller (Appendix A, Table 32). Presumably the younger persons who were the most recent college graduates were the ones most likely to move, if for no other reason than that they were not firmly implanted in jobs in the South. Most of the older persons, on the other hand, had job, family, and other connections already established in the South, and hence many fewer migrated to other parts of the country.

Another indication of migration of college graduates during the 1960's is afforded by the previously cited Louisiana study. Of those employed in the Fall of 1965, about one and a half years after graduation, nearly 6 out of 10 of the men and over 7 out of 10 of the women were working in Louisiana. Small proportions of both men and women were working in other parts of the South. But the central point is that under 3 in 10 of the men and only a little over 1 in 10 of the women had secured employment out of the South. Comparison of location of the first job following graduation with that held in the Fall of 1965 suggests that as time passed, the proportion securing employment out of the South increased modestly. But the strong inference is that the two thirds or more of the students in our study who hope to relocate out of the South probably will not do so immediately following graduation, or even within a year or two. Most will enter the labor force in their native states, and remain there for a considerable time. And the longer they remain in the South the more likely they are to continue living there, since the frequency of migration decreases with advancing age.

In summary, then, we can evaluate the probabilities of migration from the South for the 1965 Southern Negro college student. Most of them are likely to obtain in the South their first job following graduation. Whether a very small, or just a small, proportion will leave the South immediately following college graduation will depend on job opportunities elsewhere. As time passes, more and more of those who initially found jobs in the South will build up equities in them and will be less anxious to migrate. If great numbers of employment opportunities open up in the North and West, more will be tempted to migrate. But if the choice is between leaving a secure and continuing job where the person and his family are living, and migrating and seeking work elsewhere with all the insecurities inherent in such a situation, the tendency is not to migrate.

There can be considerable movement without leaving the South, of course. Civil service employment in Washington, D.C., will attract large numbers in future years. But migration from Texas or Georgia, or any other Southern state, to Washington, D.C., or Maryland or Virginia, is migration within the South. Our best estimate is that, at the most, only half of the college students who plan to leave the South will do so.

NOTES TO CHAPTER 6

1. A. J. Jaffe and Walter Adams, "Trends in College Enrollment," College Board Review, Winter, 1964-65, No. 55, pp. 27ff.

2. Kenneth B. Clark and Lawrence Plotkin, The Negro Student at Integrated Colleges (New York: National Scholarship Service and Fund for Negro Students, 1963).

3. Ibid., p. 15.

4. Ibid., p. 20.

5. Ibid., pp. 55, 56.

6. Number of persons who completed five years or more of college divided by number who had completed four years or more. Data for 1960 from U.S. Bureau of the Census. U.S. Census of Population: 1960. Educational Attainment (Final Report PC(2)5B; Washington, D.C.: U.S. Government Printing Office, 1963), Table 2.

7. Preliminary unpublished findings from a Bureau of Applied Social Research study currently in progress and supported by the U.S. Office of Education. The data were collected by the U.S. Bureau of the Census as part of the Current Population Survey.

8. Carolyn F. Husan and Michael E. Schiltz, College, Color, and Employment: Racial Differentials in Post Graduate Employment Among 1964 Graduates of Louisiana Colleges (Report No. 116; Chicago: National Opinion Research Center, University of Chicago, July, 1966).

9. Patricia Gurin and Daniel Katz, Motivation and Aspiration in the Negro College (Ann Arbor: Survey Research Center of the Institute of Social Research, 1966). This study was conducted for the Bureau of Research of the U.S. Office of Education. See especially Chapter IV, "Student Evaluations of Occupations," from which, in combination with data from our own study, we derive the conclusions presented here.

10. During the decade 1950 to 1960 the number of nonwhite men in professional and technical jobs increased much more rapidly than did the number of white men. Apparently this was due in large measure to government hiring and the fair employment practices acts. Although precise data post-1960 are not yet available, this pattern appears to have continued until at least 1965. See A. J. Jaffe and J. B. Gordon, "A Note on Occupational Mobility for White and Nonwhite Males, 1950 to 1965," The New York Statistician, 18 (December, 1966).

11. Included here are many occupations classified by the U.S. Census Bureau as "Professional, technical, and kindred workers" which do not necessarily require a college education; for example, actors, artists, athletes, dancers, draftsmen, entertainers (not elsewhere classified),

funeral embalmers and directors, musicians, re-
ligious workers except clergymen, sports instructors and officials, etc.

12. U.S. Bureau of the Census. U.S. Census
of Population: 1960. Characteristics of Teachers
(Final Report PC(2)7D; Washington, D.C.: U.S.
Government Printing Office, 1964), Table 4.

13. Husan and Schiltz, op. cit.

14. Educational Attainment, op. cit.,
Table 3.

CHAPTER **7** COLLEGES
AND
SOCIAL
CLASS

1) *Despite the extensive growth of
enrollment in primarily Negro colleges,
attendance is still highly related to
socio-economic class. The children of
middle and upper class families attend
college and, in turn, become the middle
and upper class families of the next
generation. Some children of the lower
class also manage to obtain a college
education and may eventually add to the
numbers of Negroes in the upper classes.
The absolute number of higher class Negroes
in the United States has increased during
the last couple of decades, and perhaps
longer, and is related to the increased
college attendance. What is not clear is
whether the number of Negroes in the socio-
economically higher classes has increased
more or less rapidly than has the number in
the lower class.*

2) *Of great significance for the
future Negro social class structure are the
class differences of the students at the
several types and qualities of Negro and
other colleges. The student body at the*

*elite Negro colleges has far more upper and
middle class students than does the student
body at the "poor" colleges.*

*3) It is clear that the Negro colleges
and the students they enroll are at least as
diverse as white colleges, and range from
the most excellent to the poorest. Because
of this diversity primarily Negro colleges
cannot be considered as a monolith, and
"action taken to remedy their defects."
Different types of colleges require different action programs, if any one wishes to
take action.*

CLASS DIFFERENCES IN COLLEGE ENROLLMENT

The group of students in all four-year primarily Negro colleges differs considerably from
all Southern Negro youth and their families. Many
more of the students have fathers in upper white-
collar occupations, parents who are high school or
college graduates, and families with higher incomes (Appendix A, Tables 16, 17, 18).

The occupational distribution of the students' fathers compares with that of all Southern
nonwhite males aged thirty-five to sixty-four, as
follows:

	White-Collar			Manual	Farm	Total
	Total	Upper	Lower			
Students' fathers	27	21	6	59	14	100%
Nonwhite men	9	5	4	70	21	100%

The educational distribution of the students' mothers, compared with that of all Southern nonwhite women aged thirty-five to sixty-four years, is as follows:

	Years of schooling completed					
	1-8	9-11	12	13-15	16+	Total
Students' mothers	19	29	28	9	15	100%
Nonwhite women	71	15	8	3	3	100%

Family income distribution for the students and for all Southern nonwhite families is as follows:

	Under $4000	$4000-9999	$10,000+	Total
Students' families	47	43	10	100%
Nonwhite families	67	29	4	100%

These class differences are not new and are also found among white students, and were found in the past as well.

CLASS DIFFERENCES AMONG THE NEGRO COLLEGES

Academic Abilities of Students

The primarily Negro colleges range in quality all the way from a small number of elite schools[1] to nonaccredited "poor" quality ones. In addition,

some graduates of Southern Negro high schools
enroll in junior colleges, and some in four-year
integrated ones, principally in the South.

The elite colleges receive a larger proportion of the academically best students than does
any other group of Negro colleges. Of nonwhite
high school graduates planning on going to college
(Fall, 1965), 63 per cent of those choosing an
elite college were in the upper half of the
national test-score distribution. Among those
going to four-year integrated colleges 58 per cent
were in the top half. At the other extreme, of
those planning on entering a "poor" college, or a
two-year school, less than 10 per cent were in the
top half of the national test-score distribution.

Such extreme diversities in the quality of
academic preparation for college--and possibly
in innate abilities--must be reflected in the
quality of the education which the college can
provide. A good teacher stimulates his students,
and good students stimulate their teacher.

Social Class

Students attending the elite primarily Negro
colleges come from wealthier families than do students at other types of four-year Negro institutions (Chart 7.1). The proportions from families
having income of $10,000 and over per year in 1965
are as follows:

Elite colleges . . . . 40 per cent

All "good" colleges . . . . 13 per cent

All "fair" colleges . . . . 11 per cent

"Poor" and accredited . . . 4 per cent

"Poor" and nonaccredited . . 2 per cent

Chart 7.1

Comparison of Students at Elite Versus "Poor"
Colleges, Selected Characteristics

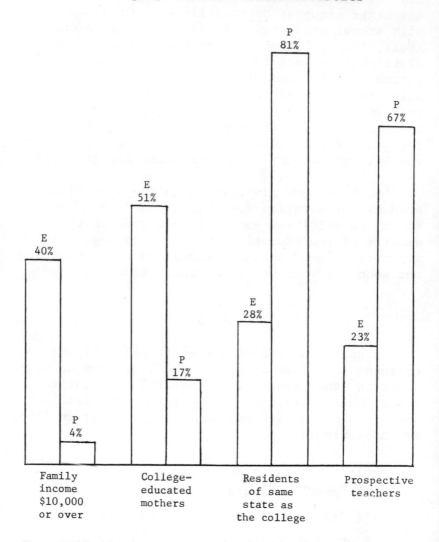

E - Students at academically highly selective, or
    elite, "good" quality colleges
F - Students at accredited, but "poor" quality,
    colleges

For all U.S. college students, the proportion
of families with income of $10,000 and over in
1960 was 41 per cent, the same as for the families
of the elite Negro students.[2] Similarly, the parents of students at the elite colleges have more
education. The proportions of college-educated
mothers of students are as follows:

Elite colleges . . . . 51 per cent

All "good" colleges . . . . 31 per cent

All "fair" colleges . . . . 23 per cent

"Poor" and accredited . . . 17 per cent

"Poor" and nonaccredited . . 15 per cent

Geographic Origin

The elite colleges attract students from all
over the United States and from foreign countries.
Only a small proportion of their students graduated from a high school in the same state in which
the college is located; the student body at the
elite colleges is far more cosmopolitan than that
of other colleges. The proportions of the students at these elite colleges who graduated from
a high school in a different state from the one
in which the college is located, or from a foreign
country, are as follows:

Elite colleges . . . . 72 per cent

All "good" colleges . . . . 43 per cent

All "fair" colleges . . . . 26 per cent

"Poor" and accredited . . . 19 per cent

"Poor" and nonaccredited . . 9 per cent

STUDENT ASPIRATIONS

Less than a quarter of the students at the elite colleges plan to teach, and the majority of them plan to become college teachers. At the other extreme, two thirds of the students at both the nonaccredited and accredited "poor" colleges plan to teach, and only a very small minority aspire to college teaching. Most students at Negro colleges hope to enter teaching at the primary and secondary levels, since they believe that these are the white-collar jobs most easily obtained. Students at the elite colleges, however, feel confident of employment in a wide variety of upper white-collar occupations to which most Negro college students do not aspire. The academic superiority and the socio-economic advantage of the elite students argue that their aspirations are realistic.

CONCLUSIONS

The students at the elite primarily Negro colleges are very different from those attending the academically poorer colleges. The former come from wealthier homes throughout the United States, the parents have had more education, and the students themselves are much better prepared for college study than are the students enrolled in the "poor" or "fair" colleges. Whether the students at the elite colleges are innately brighter or more intelligent than other students at Negro colleges cannot be determined from the test scores alone. What we do know is that the combination of more educated and financially richer parents results in a student body better prepared to receive a better college education. Very probably the elite students will surmount occupational and other racial barriers in later life far more frequently than students attending other colleges.

NOTES TO CHAPTER 7

1. See Appendix C for further explanation.

2. Rexford G. Moon, Jr., "A Model for Deter-
mining Future Student Aid Needs in the United
States for the Support of Full-Time Undergraduate
Education," duplicated, 1964, Table 5, p. 12.

CHAPTER **8** THE SOUTHERN
NEGRO COLLEGE
STUDENT AND
PUBLIC JUNIOR
COLLEGES

*1) Where public junior colleges are
available, they attract large numbers of
Negro students. One important feature is
the low cost to the student; a second is
the ease of admission.*

*2) In the mid-1960's the potential
Negro college population tended to live in
states which have few public junior colleges. This lack of availability cur-
tailed potential attendance at the public
two-year schools.*

*3) During the 1960's, however, many
states were expanding their public junior
college facilities greatly. By the mid-
1970's a much larger proportion of the
Southern Negro youth will have public
colleges available to them.*

*4) The evidence suggests that as of
the mid-1960's, the public two-year schools
were not taking students away from the
Negro four-year colleges. Instead, they*

*seemed to attract many students who other-
wise might not have gone to any college.*

    *5) The type of student who attends
the two-year college resembles the type
attending the "poor" Negro four-year ones.
If, with the expansion of the public
junior colleges, students will in fact be
drawn away from Negro four-year colleges,
perhaps the "poor" colleges will lose
students, although they are the schools
which are now planning to expand most
rapidly.*

GROWTH OF THE TWO-YEAR COLLEGE

In the course of the last half century the
public junior college has had by far the greatest
rate of growth of all major types of colleges and
universities in this country (Chart 8.1). In
1920, just after the end of World War I, only
about 3,000 students attended a total of ten such
schools. The 1965 estimated enrollment was very
nearly 700,000 students, attending perhaps 400
institutions.[1] In that year about 14 per cent of
all college students were enrolled in public
junior colleges, and these two-year schools received about 25 per cent of new college entrants.

There still are (as of the mid-1960's) large
numbers of private two-year colleges, but they
enroll only a small proportion of all junior college students. In 1949 there were about 200,000
students in all two-year colleges, of which about
30 per cent were enrolled in private ones; by 1965
only 15 per cent were in private schools. The
establishment of many new public junior colleges
accounts for the great increase in the total number of these institutions. Accordingly, when we
speak of students enrolled in junior colleges in
the mid-1960's, it should be remembered that most
of them are in public rather than private colleges.

Chart 8.1

Total National Enrollment in Two-Year
Public Colleges, 1920-1965

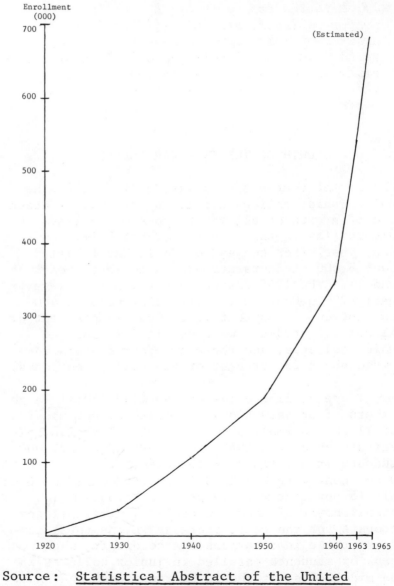

Source: <u>Statistical Abstract of the United
          States, 1966</u>, Tables 180 and 184.

100

WHO GOES TO JUNIOR COLLEGES?

These colleges, in comparison with four-year institutions, attract relatively more students who score lower on tests, who come from families in which the head is a blue-collar worker, and from poorer families.

Among all U.S. high school graduates in 1960 who entered college that Fall,[2] we find the following I.Q. test scores:

	Four-year colleges	Two-year colleges
	%	%
Top half	89	62
Bottom half	11	38
Total	100	100

The occupations of the heads of households from which these students came were as follows:

	Four-year colleges	Two-year colleges
	%	%
White-collar workers	59	47
Blue-collar workers, including unemployed and not in labor force (but excluding agriculture)	34	51
Agriculture	7	2
Total	100	100

Family income is related to occupation, and blue-collar workers tend to earn less than white-collar workers. Since more of the two-year college students, in comparison with those enrolled in four-year ones, come from blue-collar families, they tend to have lower incomes, as follows:

	Four-year colleges	Two-year colleges
	%	%
Under $6,000 per year	36	40
$6,000 and over per year	64	60
Total	100	100

With regard to I.Q. tests, those who enrolled in two-year colleges resemble the high school graduates who did not enter college in the Fall of 1960. Among these latter graduates, 53 per cent were in the upper half of the I.Q. test scores, as compared with 62 per cent who entered junior colleges (and 89 per cent who entered four-year institutions).

In class standing in high school, the two-year college entrants and those not planning on college resembled each other even more closely-- 43 per cent of the former and 41 per cent of the latter group were in the top half of the distribution, in contrast to 78 per cent of the four-year college entrants.[3] Since the student's high school record is a major academic criterion for admission to four-year colleges, the two-year colleges apparently admit students with unimpressive high school records; many of them presumably would not qualify for four-year colleges. Thus it would appear that the two-year colleges tend to attract many who might not otherwise have attended a senior college.

Since the junior colleges tend to attract
more of the financially poorer students and those
who have scored lower on tests, we may infer that
these colleges tend to attract a somewhat different type of student than does the four-year
school. Presumably the two-year ones are only
partly in competition for new entrants with the
four-year colleges.

Some additional information is available from
the college plans of the Negro high school
seniors. Among all high school seniors living in
the states of Florida, Texas, and Mississippi
(which have many public junior colleges), 35 per
cent were reported as entering college. However,
among those seniors graduating from Southern
states which had but few public two-year colleges,
only 25 per cent were reported as entering college. This suggests that the availability of free
public institutions attracts some 10 per cent of
the high school graduates who otherwise might not
have entered college.

This finding is confirmed by the information
on all U.S. high school graduates. Among those
who graduated in June, 1960:

32 per cent entered four-year colleges,

 9 per cent entered two-year colleges, and

59 per cent did not enter any college, by
        the Fall of 1960.

Among those who graduated from high school in
June, 1966:[4]

35 per cent entered four-year colleges,

17 per cent entered two-year colleges, and

43 per cent did not enter any college, by
        the Fall of 1966.

Comparison of these entry rates for 1960 and
1966 shows clearly that the great increase in
college going was largely at the junior college
level. The proportion who entered two-year colleges almost doubled, and increased about 8 percentage points. However, there was an estimated
increase of only about 3 percentage points in the
proportion enrolling in four-year colleges. We
may infer (although we cannot test this inference
empirically) that in the absence of an expanding
junior college system, there would have been a
much smaller increase for this six-year period in
the total numbers "attending college."

THE PUBLIC JUNIOR COLLEGES

The public junior colleges are in a strong
competitive position for attracting many of the
prospective undergraduates, especially the less
affluent. They are the least costly of all types
of colleges, not only because of low or nonexistent tuition, but also because they are almost all
commuter schools. In addition, entrance requirements are the least demanding; the usual requirement is simply high school graduation. In most
instances these colleges have been deliberately
located in centers of population, and are consequently immediately available to large numbers of
high school graduates. These institutions are
especially attractive to Southern Negro high
school seniors.

In terms of their cost and entrance requirements, the primarily Negro colleges are generally
easier for Negroes to attend than are other types
of four-year colleges, but in comparison with the
public junior colleges they are indeed expensive,
and many of them are relatively selective. In
theory, at least, public junior colleges might
very well replace the primarily Negro colleges as
the initial avenue to a college degree for
Southern Negro youth. Presumably the junior
college student could have two additional years to

surmount deficiencies in his high school preparation for advanced study, as well as to secure financing of two years of senior college. On the other hand, for some students the two years of junior college would represent the extent of their higher educational aspirations.

Officially these schools are open to Negro applicants in all the Southern states where they exist. We do not know to what extent Negro students are unwilling to attend them because of complex social reasons related to the Southern problem of race relations. Earl McGrath[5] reports that there is often a very strong feeling of achievement for both the student and his family when he "goes away" to a four-year college, even to a mediocre one. For many students a local two-year college may not be an acceptable substitute, and they will not plan to attend college at all.

Nevertheless, even if these complex social reasons do exert an influence, large numbers of nonwhites do go--or plan on going--to junior colleges. Indeed, for the total United States it is clear that nonwhites plan on attending junior colleges to the same or a larger extent than do whites. The types of college specified by those 1965 high school seniors with college plans for the Fall of 1966 were as follows:[6]

	High school seniors	
	White	Nonwhite
	%	%
Two-year college only	22	23
Two- and four-year college	21	34
Total two-year colleges	*43*	*57*
Four-year college only	57	43
All plans	100	100

Amost identical proportions of white and non-white seniors (22 and 23 per cent, respectively) look forward only to junior college. Another 21 per cent of the whites hope to transfer to a four-year college and receive a baccalaureate, but a significantly larger proportion of the nonwhites (34 per cent) expect to do so. However, more whites than nonwhites plan to enter initially a four-year college.

It appears that many Negroes who hope to complete four years of college are forced by economic and academic reasons to enter a two-year college, with the expectation of transferring to a senior college to complete their studies. We do not know how many of them actually do so, but the reports of high dropout rates from junior colleges and low transfer rates to senior colleges suggest that many of these students will fail to realize their ambitions.

Of the 1965 Southern Negro high school graduates whom we studied, about 1 in 8 of those planning to enter college in the Fall of 1966 hoped to attend a public junior college, almost all in the South (Appendix A, Table 9). Although this proportion is considerably smaller than the national data just cited, it does not negate the argument that junior colleges, *where they are available*, are at least as attractive to nonwhites as to whites.

AVAILABILITY AND NEGRO ENROLLMENT

In 1965 there were 102 public junior colleges in the sixteen states of the South and Southwest; eighty-three were located in four states--Florida, Texas, Mississippi, and Oklahoma.[7] Quite clearly the "junior college movement" had not as yet penetrated the majority of the Southern states, and in consequence the opportunity for Southern Negro high school graduates to enter these schools is

limited. In a fifth state, North Carolina, there
were only three public junior colleges, but one of
these was a large school created by the merging of
a formerly white with a formerly Negro school, and
it enrolled a considerable number of Negro high
school graduates from this state.

The students in our 1965 sample who attended
high school in states with large numbers of junior
colleges were the ones most likely to plan on
entering such two-year schools. The proportions
are as follows:

	%		%
Florida	63	Oklahoma	8
Mississippi	39	North Carolina	5
Texas	24	All other states in our sample of high school students	under 0.5

In the Pacific coast states—particularly
California and Washington—where there are many
public junior colleges, over 7 in 10 of all Negro
college students were enrolled in them.

Our broad conclusion is that considerable
proportions of Southern Negro high school seniors
select public junior colleges if, and *only if*,
they are geographically readily available (Chart
8.2). For the five states separately tabulated
we cannot explain, from the information we
possess, just why the proportions vary to such an
extent. Undoubtedly this is a complex matter involving the numbers of junior colleges, their
locations within each state, the sizes and locations of the Negro high school populations relative to the locations of the colleges, and perhaps

Chart 8.2

Attendance at and Availability of
Junior Colleges, by Region

(a) Proportions of All Negro and White
Degree-Credit Undergraduates Enrolled in
College Who Were Attending Public Junior
Colleges, by Region, October, 1965

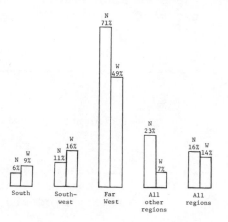

(b) Number of Public Junior Colleges, 1965,
by Regions, and for Selected States

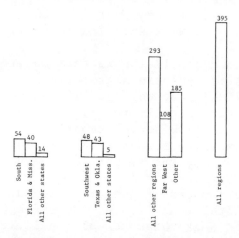

Sources: See Appendix A, Tables 41 and 42.

the extent to which social forces encourage racial
integration in the various states.

In general, the potential college population
of white students in the United States is distributed geographically more nearly according to
the availability of public two-year colleges than
is the potential nonwhite college population, and
the ability of the nonwhites to attend such
schools is minimized. The geographic distribution
of the white and nonwhite high school seniors in
1960, and of the public junior colleges in 1965,
was as follows:

	Public junior colleges	High school seniors	
		White	Nonwhite
	%	%	%
South Atlantic	11.9	11.6	27.6
East South Central	4.8	5.7	12.9
West South Central	10.9	8.6	13.9
Total South	*27.6*	*25.9*	*54.4*
Middle Atlantic	9.1	20.0	14.0
East North Central	15.0	20.4	13.2
Pacific	23.4	12.6	12.7
New England, West North Central, and Mountain	24.9	21.1	5.7
Total non-South	*72.4*	*74.1*	*45.6*
All regions	100.0	100.0	100.0

It is also true that in the South and Southwest, where availability was low, smaller proportions of Negro than of white college students were
attending public junior colleges, 8 versus 12 per
cent. In the Far West, where availability of
schools was high, far larger proportions of Negro
than of white college students were attending
these junior colleges, 71 versus 49 per cent.[8]
To be sure, far larger proportions of both white
and nonwhite students were attending public junior
colleges in the Far West than in the South and
Southwest, but the difference is considerably
greater in the case of the Negro students. We
infer that once public junior colleges are well
established as a higher educational fixture in a
region, they are particularly attractive to Negro
college aspirants by virtue of their low cost and
lenient admissions requirements. Very possibly
this effect has been minimized to some extent
in the few Southern states where many of these
schools exist by the availability of primarily
Negro colleges, and perhaps by strong social
pressures toward segregated higher education, but
it is still evident that large proportions of
Southern Negro youth are attracted to public
junior colleges in the Southern states where they
are available.

POSSIBLE EXPANSION OF PUBLIC JUNIOR
COLLEGES IN THE SOUTH

Since availability of these schools is so
important in determining whether Negro students
will choose them, it is pertinent to ask whether
there will be a large extension of these two-year
colleges in the near future. In 1965, Florida had
twenty-three junior colleges, Georgia eight, Maryland twelve, Mississippi seventeen, Oklahoma
twelve, Texas thirty-one, North Carolina three,
and there was one each in West Virginia, Kentucky,
and Alabama. There is clearly room for great

expansion in many of the Southern states, if their
legislators so desire.

Since 1965 (and as of mid-1967)[9] the following occurred or is in prospect, to the best of
our knowledge:

Alabama	Fourteen public junior colleges, most of which opened in 1965 as a group. They are officially integrated, but the actual integration status is in considerable doubt.
Georgia	Eleven public junior colleges which are part of the university system, but may become independent. This is a modest expansion.
Virginia	Plans made and legislation enacted for a network of public junior colleges.
North Carolina	A large network, formed by converting "education centers" into public junior colleges.
Maryland	A modest continuing expansion in line with past development.
Kentucky	Ten public junior colleges under the state university system.

The following Southern states, then, are not
likely to have large numbers of public junior
colleges within the next decade: Delaware, West
Virginia, South Carolina, Tennessee, Arkansas,
Louisiana, and Oklahoma. About 28 per cent of all

Southern and border state nonwhite high school
seniors in 1960 lived in these states. This,
then, is the approximate proportion of students
who are not likely to have access to a public
junior college within the next decade. We judge
this from the historical observation that there
is almost a decade between the time a state
decides to open a junior college system and the
time that a significant number of such schools
are actually in operation.[10]

PUBLIC JUNIOR COLLEGES AND THE
FOUR-YEAR NEGRO COLLEGE

There seems to be little competition between
these two types of school as of the mid-1960's.
The public junior colleges apparently attract
large numbers of students who otherwise probably
would not have entered college. We judge this
from the observation that the three Southern
states with large public two-year college systems
enrolled about 35 per cent of the June, 1960,
Southern Negro high school graduating class, as
compared with 25 per cent in those states which
had but few public junior colleges.

Comparison of the numbers of new entries into
four-year Negro colleges between 1962 and 1965 for
these two groups of states shows that college enrollment in both increased greatly. Indeed, the
number of new entries into the four-year Negro
colleges in Florida, Texas, and Mississippi (the
states with large numbers of public junior colleges) increased by 33 per cent between 1962 and
1965, whereas in the other states the increase was
only 21 per cent. These data suggest that the
four-year Negro college is at least holding its
own vis-à-vis the public junior college.

In Florida, Texas, and Mississippi, where
there are many public junior colleges, somewhat

fewer Negro high school graduates in those states
in 1965 expected to enter four-year Negro colleges. The proportions were as follows:

	Florida, Texas, Mississippi	Other South
	%	%
Entering:		
Two-year colleges	15	1
Four-year Negro colleges	17	21
Other four-year colleges	3	3
Not entering college	65	75
Total	100	100

In the states having fewer junior colleges, 4 per
cent more of the high school graduates in 1965
were slated to enter four-year Negro colleges.
About the same per cent were to enter other four-
year colleges, in the South or elsewhere. This
finding seems to suggest that the public junior
college may be taking students away from the Negro
four-year ones. However, such a conclusion is too
uncertain on the basis of the information available for the following reasons:

  a) No one knows how many students who first
enroll in two-year colleges will subsequently
transfer to four-year Negro colleges. It will be
recalled that over half of the nonwhite high
school seniors (interviewed in total United States
in the Fall of 1965) who said that they planned on
entering a junior college, also planned on
attending a senior college.

b)   Perhaps very many of those who enroll in two-year schools would not have completed four years of study even if they had first enrolled in four-year Negro colleges. The potential college dropout may tend to enroll in the junior college.

c)   Perhaps the four-year Negro colleges in Florida, Texas, and Mississippi do not have sufficient capacity to admit all qualified applicants, so that many had to turn to two-year schools.

NOTES TO CHAPTER 8

1. U.S. Bureau of the Census, Statistical Abstract, 1966 (Washington, D.C., 1967), Table 180, p. 129.

There are two major sources of statistics on junior colleges, the U.S. Office of Education and the American Association of Junior Colleges. The statistics of the Office of Education predate those of the Association by some years, and so are more useful for studying long-term trends. In this chapter we use the Office of Education data when our questions are historical ones. The Association figures, because of fuller coverage of the total of junior colleges, are more appropriate for determining very recent developments. The Association reports larger numbers of junior colleges, and larger numbers of students enrolled, than does the Office of Education. The difference in coverage stems in part from the fact that the Office does not report two-year branches or affiliates of state universities as separate colleges. These branches function as independent schools in most ways that affect their students. The Association reports them separately. In several Southern states public junior colleges are established within the state university complex, and there are considerable numbers of such branches. We therefore communicated with the

Association to determine very recent trends in the
Southern states, and our data on such trends and
their implications for the future, which appear
toward the end of this chapter, derive from information given us by the Association.

2. Preliminary unpublished findings from a
Bureau of Applied Social Research study currently
in progress and supported by the U.S. Office of
Education. The data were collected by the U.S.
Bureau of the Census as part of the Current Popu-
lation Survey.

3. Ibid., and U.S. Bureau of the Census,
"Factors Related to College Attendance of Farm and
Nonfarm High School Graduates: 1960," Farm Population (Series Census-ERS [P-27], No. 32, June 15,
1962.

4. Preliminary unpublished findings from a
Bureau of Applied Social Research study, op. cit.,
subject to revision.

5. Earl J. McGrath, The Predominantly Negro
College in Transition (New York: Teachers College,
Columbia University, 1965). See especially Chap-
ter 3, "Student Costs and Admissions Policies."

6. Preliminary unpublished findings from a
Bureau of Applied Social Research study, op. cit.

7. Derived from data collected by the U.S.
Office of Education.

8. Statistics computed from James S.
Coleman, et al., Equality of Educational Opportunity (Washington, D.C.: U.S. Office of Education, 1966), Table 5.5.5.

9. Communication from the American Association of Junior Colleges, Washington, D.C. (June,
1967).

10. Our model here is the State of Florida. About ten years elapsed between the date when a survey of the need for public junior colleges was officially ordered and the date when an extensive complex of such schools, enrolling many thousands of students, was in full operation.

CHAPTER **9** PROJECTIONS
TO 1975 OF
HIGH SCHOOL
GRADUATES
BY STATES

*By 1975 the number of Southern Negro
youth (aged eighteen to twenty-four) who
will be high school graduates will probably
double as a minimum. The maximum is likely
to be more than triple the number in 1960,
when about 350,000 persons graduated from
high school. By 1975 the number should increase to at least 624,000, and perhaps to
well over 1 million.*

*The minimum increase will result en-
tirely from population growth. The maximum
number will be the result of population
growth plus increased proportions of students who finish high school.*

*College attendance should increase at
least as much as high school graduation.
How many of these 1975 youth will be
attending primarily Negro colleges in the
South, however, we do not know.*

Our projections of Southern Negro high school
graduates to 1975 by states (both the absolute

117

number of such graduates in that year, and the per cent changes from 1960*) have been made on the assumption that no major depression will occur and that this country will not become engaged in an "all out" war. Of the various factors (other than war or depression) that can materially affect trends in educational attainment, the demographic factor can be estimated relatively more precisely, based as it is on past birth rates, and trends in migration into and out of the South.

Another factor is the complex of attitudes toward education, perhaps most clearly expressed in public policies and provisions favoring, to a greater or a lesser extent, advances in educational attainment. Such attitudes and consequent policies in regard to education can change considerably in a brief space of time. For example, it is difficult to say whether Federal aid to students attending colleges will decrease, remain the same, or increase in the next few years, and what the extent of any such changes will be.

There was great variation in the proportions of nonwhite** youth who completed high school in 1960, ranging from 18.2 per cent in Mississippi to 48.5 per cent in the District of Columbia.[1] On the basis of this information and the two population projections (ages eighteen to twenty-four) for each state,[2] four sets of projected numbers of high school graduates were made:

a) The *lowest* projection assumes that in each state in 1975 the same proportion of eighteen

_____

*See Appendix E for detailed discussion of the methodology.

**The data presented are for total nonwhites; in these Southern states almost all of the nonwhites are Negro.

to twenty-four year olds will have graduated from
high school as was observed among nonwhite youth
in the state in 1960, and there will be the *least*
population growth.

b)   The *next* assumes that the same proportion
will graduate from high school in 1975, and there
will be the *most* population growth.

c)   The *next to the highest* projection
assumes that in each state in 1975 the proportion
of eighteen- to twenty-four-year-old nonwhites who
will have graduated from high school will equal
the proportion observed among white youth in that
state in 1960, and there will be the *least* population growth.

d)   The *highest* projection assumes that in
1975 the proportion who will have graduated from
high school will equal that of white youth in
1960, and there will be the *most* population
growth.

We have no "best estimate" as to which 1975
projection is most likely to occur. On the one
hand, we believe that there will be substantial
increases in the proportion of Negro youth who
will have graduated from high school. If the
reader wishes to assume that by 1975 a larger
proportion of the Negroes will have graduated
from high school than we assume as the maximum
(by taking the graduation rates of white youth
in 1960), he need but increase our maximum figure
by whatever he desires.

On the other hand, we cannot even guess at
the amount of migration out of the South which
will occur by 1975. The Census Bureau, when
making the population projections, allowed for
out-migration, but until the 1970 census count is
available, no one will know how accurately the
volume of out-migration--state by state--was
estimated.

Numbers of Nonwhite High School Graduates in 1960
and Estimated Numbers in 1975, by States*

(numbers in thousands)

State	1960 no.	1975 estimate				Minimum % increase	Maximum % increase
		Lowest	2	3	Highest		
Alabama	28.1	47	49	80	83	67	195
Arkansas	7.8	14	15	31	33	79	323
District of Columbia	19.2	37	39	61	63	93	228
Florida	40.7	78	81	97	100	92	146
Georgia	29.1	48	50	100	103	65	254
Louisiana	28.3	51	52	103	106	80	275
Maryland	18.2	36	37	59	61	98	235
Mississippi	15.0	26	27	84	89	73	493
Missouri	14.0	28	28	44	44	100	214
North Carolina	37.3	64	66	105	109	72	191
South Carolina	19.5	32	34	72	76	64	290
Tennessee	18.5	34	35	51	52	84	181
Texas	46.7	87	87	118	119	86	155
Virginia	24.3	42	43	76	77	73	217
Total	346.7	624	643	1081	1115	80	222

*Omitted from this table are the following Southern states: Delaware, Kentucky, Oklahoma, and West Virginia. The Census Bureau presented no 1975 estimates for them because they each had under 250,000 nonwhites in 1960. In 1960 these states had only 20,548 nonwhite youth 18 to 24 years of age who had graduated from high school.

An alternate set of projections for the
total of the fourteen states is presented in
Appendix E. These projections have the advantage
of being based on trends in educational attainment at three different levels, 1940–1960. They
have the disadvantage of not presenting figures
for the individual states.

NOTES TO CHAPTER 9

1. U.S. Bureau of the Census. U.S. Census
of Population: 1960. Detailed Characteristics,
United States Summary, Final Report PC(1)D
(Washington, D.C.: U.S. Government Printing
Office, 1961), Tables 101 and 102 for the appro-
priate states.

2. The population projections are taken
from U.S. Bureau of the Census, "Illustrative
Projections of the Population of States: 1970 to
1985," Current Population Reports ("Population
Estimates," Series P-25, No. 326, February, 1966),
Table 7, pp. 86–88.

CHAPTER **10** MAJOR
FINDINGS
AND
THEIR POLICY
IMPLICATIONS

*There are precisely two clusters of
significant findings which emerge from our
study of the Negro colleges and the students they enroll:*

*1) Most of these colleges are either
academically "poor" or very questionable
in quality, and they enroll students who
are predominantly ill-prepared for college-
level work. The value of an education at
these colleges for such students appears
slight. In turn, it seems highly unlikely
that the college experience would particularly enhance the student's later con-
tribution to his community.*

*2) These conditions will continue to
be the case--and probably will hold true
for considerably larger numbers of stu-
dents--in the foreseeable future, unless
concerted contravening measures are brought
to bear upon the problem.*

THE FINDINGS

Growth in Enrollment

All the evidence indicates that the primarily
Negro college will continue its long historical
growth from only a few thousand students enrolled
in the early years of this century to over 100,000
in 1965. This rate of growth at least parallels,
and very possibly exceeds, that of all college
enrollments in the United States during the same
span of years. By the mid-1970's the anticipated
increase in the numbers of Southern Negro high
school graduates--the candidates for these col-
leges--should assure large increases in enrollments.

Long-term and short-term historical trends in
enrollments in Negro colleges, the expectations of
the college officials, and projections based on
population growth and trends in educational
attainment all appear to concur. By 1975 the number of Southern Negroes who may be high school
graduates is likely to increase by 150 per cent or
more--from over 300,000 in 1960 to well over
700,000 in 1975. There will be, of course, great
variation from one state to another. Consequently, college enrollment will also increase
greatly, and if the observed trends continue, we
would expect much of this growth to be in the primarily Negro colleges in the South.

Most of the Negro colleges are academically
unselective. Many of them, moreover, are organized to meet, through remedial and other special
programs, the particular scholastic needs of the
Southern Negro high school graduate; there is
little evidence that Southern Negro youth will
soon overcome their relatively poor primary and
secondary schooling. In consequence, though the
social and legal barriers to attendance at integrated colleges may continue to crumble, the

academic barriers appear likely to endure. Poorly
prepared Negro high school graduates in the South
will probably continue to turn to the Negro colleges for higher education.

It is also predictable that the number of
public junior colleges--expense-free or inexpensive commuter colleges with extremely liberal
admissions policies--will increase significantly
in the South by 1970, and that many more Negro
students will enroll in them. Swift expansion of
these public junior colleges could slow down the
rate of growth of the four-year predominantly
Negro colleges, but it is difficult to estimate
the extent to which the enrollment at the two-year
schools would cut into that of these four-year
colleges. With the large growth in the numbers
of potential college students, there may be room
for considerable growth of both the four-year primarily Negro college and the public two-year institution.

The Students

The great majority of students who attend the
primarily Negro four-year colleges are of Southern
origin and natives of the state in which their
college is located. They come from high socio-
economic backgrounds relative to all Southern
Negro youth, but low ones relative to Southern
white youth. The great majority attend Negro
primary and secondary schools and stand high in
their classes. On the other hand, their performance on achievement tests is poor relative to that
of all students throughout the country. Over the
years more girls than boys enrolled in the primarily Negro colleges.

Virtually all of these college students would
like white-collar jobs, and the great majority
want to enter upper white-collar professions. Few
aspire to become clerical and sales workers, or

managers, officials, and proprietors; most students feel that there is little job opportunity
for Negroes in these occupations. The majority
hope to teach, chiefly at the primary and secondary levels, and large proportions accordingly
major in education. There is considerable evidence that career aspirations center about occupations for which the students feel, correctly or
not, the least disadvantage relative to white
competitors with equivalent preparation.

The great majority are full-time degree-
credit students who enter college following completion of high school college-preparatory
courses. About 8 in 10 hope to enter graduate
or professional school; this indicates that nearly
all hope to complete the full four years of college. Very probably all of the students hoping to
be professional and technical workers are aware of
the necessity of finishing college, and the de-
sirability of graduate work for entry into the
professions.

These plans appear relatively realistic if,
and only if, they complete the full four years of
college. Historically hardly half of Negro college entrants have done so. Of those who do
graduate, perhaps as many as half will continue in
graduate or professional school. Most of the college graduates--between 80 and 90 per cent--will
obtain professional employment. On the other
hand, most of those who become college dropouts
will not obtain upper white-collar jobs. About
half of the students wish to become teachers, and
it is very likely that this proportion of the college graduates will succeed in doing so.

It is likely that most of the Negro students
will obtain their initial employment in the South,
principally in the state where they attended college. About two thirds of the students hope to
leave the South after graduation, but the majority
will not do so immediately. Although historically

there was considerable out-migration of better
educated Negroes, this exodus occurred some time
after completing college study. The ultimate
volume of out-migration will depend on job opportunities in the North and West, relative to the
South; as of the mid-1960's this is an unpredict-
able factor.

A small number of elite students--elite both
in terms of academic performance and upper socio-
economic backgrounds--attend a minority of schools
within the category of "good" colleges. These
students are about as affluent as the average
white student attending college, and on the average somewhat more able. They aspire to lives that
are markedly different from those anticipated by
all other Negro college students. Few plan to
teach; the majority plan to enter occupations
which most other students apparently perceive as
unrealistic goals. These elite students evince
the clear and positive relationships between a
favorable socio-economic position, better academic
performance, and more ambitious plans for the
future.

The Colleges

A little over half of the students who attend
primarily Negro colleges are enrolled in public
four-year institutions, and a little under half in
private four-year ones. Only a small residual
number enroll in private two-year schools; since
these schools appear to serve special educational
purposes in most cases, meaningful comparison with
the senior colleges is not possible. In the
recent past, almost all of the formerly segregated
two-year public colleges have been officially "integrated" with local white counterparts, particularly in Florida, where public two-year colleges
are very prevalent. There are now very few, if
any, primarily Negro public junior colleges.

Just over 6 in 20 students attend "good"
colleges, just under 9 in 20 attend "fair" ones,
and just over 5 in 20 "poor" ones. Although the
better colleges attract better students, not all
can enroll in such schools since the opportunity
to attend a "good" college depends to a considerable extent on where a student lives. Therefore,
since few students appear to be financially able
to enroll in college far from their homes, few
leave the "deep South" to go to "good" colleges
elsewhere. Nevertheless, considerable proportions
of the better high school graduates from the "deep
South" do enroll in better colleges located in
other states. On the other hand, few students of
any quality from outside the "deep South" enter
colleges in that region, where there are only five
relatively small and "good" colleges.

The single most important finding is that the
"poor" colleges appear to be the ones which have
been increasing their enrollments, and especially
their new entrants, the most in the recent past.
Expansion has been somewhat less rapid for the
"fair" colleges, and least rapid of all quality
groups for the "good" colleges. These findings
apply especially to colleges in the "deep South."
The few "good" colleges in this sub-region appear
to have had negligible increases in their total of
new entrants, 1962-1965, whereas the "poor" colleges had an increase of almost 50 per cent.
Apparently it is the less selective, less expensive "poor" college that has been increasingly
attracting the mounting number of Southern Negro
high school graduates hoping to enter college.
Accordingly, it is the "poor" college that seems
to be intensifying its recruitment efforts.

The recent increase of Federal student loan
and work-study funds is probably responsible, to
a considerable extent, for these trends. This
financial assistance is available to students
attending all types and qualities of recognized

colleges, and presumably has enabled many lower
socio-economic students, and those with less adequate academic records, to enter college. Many
such students may decide in favor of the less
expensive, less selective, academically poorer
colleges where increased Federal student aid more
than compensates for the somewhat lesser college-
financed scholarship aid available. We assume
that continuation of these trends depends largely
on future educational policies and programs, including the availability of Federal funds.

IMPLICATIONS AND RECOMMENDATIONS

That these findings call "for concerted
action against a well-entrenched foe" may be
stimulating rhetoric, but rhetoric alone will not
bring down the walls of twentieth century Jericho.
Accordingly, we are outlining a program which is
implied in the findings, and which can be carried
out. For the sake of convenience we will consider
the Negro colleges, their students, and the elementary and secondary students separately, even
though all three are essentially facets of a
single educational problem.

As preface to the remarks to follow, it
should be stated that we feel that the primarily
Negro college will gradually lose its principal
role in the education of the Negro unless it
should be maintained by simple ethnocentrism.
The social forces are working toward more, rather
than less, integration. Public colleges are
growing more rapidly than private institutions,
and the public ones tend to be more nearly integrated, even in the South. On the other hand,
for a variety of reasons, including inertia, the
existing primarily Negro colleges will continue
well into the future. Hence, in thinking a
generation or two ahead, we must simultaneously

consider policy with regard to the existing primarily Negro colleges, and policy aimed at helping
Negro youth--today and in the future--to adapt
themselves better to the world outside the ghetto.
For it is this outside world which is moulding the
future Negro's educational requirements. As long
as the professional or business man was satisfied
to remain and work exclusively in the ghetto where
he was sheltered, to at least some extent, from
outside competition, the quality of his education
vis-a-vis that of his possible competitors was not
particularly relevant. Once he leaves the ghetto,
as so many are now trying to do, his education
must be of sufficient quality so that he can hold
his own against white competition.

The Colleges

Public Junior and "Poor" Negro Colleges

We believe that there should be no escalation
of moneys or efforts expended on improving the
"poor" colleges or the great majority of the
"fair" colleges because these schools do not
appear to be amenable to improvement in a reasonable span of time or at a reasonable cost. We
would except those "fair" colleges which may
possess the potential for improvement without
excessive expenditures, should such colleges in
fact exist. Instead, the moneys and efforts
available should be devoted to broad and swift
expansion of a network of integrated public two-
year colleges throughout the South. Emphasis, of
course, should be on geographic areas where there
are few or no such schools today; they should be
located in centers of population, white and Negro,
and should be low-cost commuter schools. The
states of California and Florida, among others,
offer approximate models for such public junior
college systems. The individual junior colleges

would be organized, in terms of their curriculum,
to serve the employment needs of the areas in
which they were located. Also, as in California,
the junior colleges would be part of a larger integrated higher educational complex. The transfer
route to senior college would be clearly mapped
for students for whom transfer would be appropriate. For students not transferring, contacts with
such agencies as state employment services should
be close.

Public junior colleges are particularly
attractive to academically less able, and socio-
economically less fortunate, students--precisely
the students who now enter the poorer Negro colleges. For persons with ideological concerns,
such public junior colleges would be integrated
schools. Integration, of course, would have
practical advantages as well as ideological ones.
In general, the poorer the Negro college, the more
totally Negro is its student body. Such segre-
gation not only isolates the student from meaningful relations with the white community, but also
represents one of the salient aspects of the pro-
vincialism of the poorer Negro colleges, as compared to the relative cosmopolitanism of the
better of these schools.

Furthermore, approximately half of those who
enter college fail to complete four years of
study. For whatever reasons, large numbers of
students remain in college for a few months only,
a year or two perhaps. For these students the
two-year college can provide all the formal post-
high school education they desire. Nothing is
gained--either by the college or the student--if
such students enroll in a four-year college only
to become college dropouts.

We are convinced that the academically less
able or less motivated Negro high school students
would attend public junior colleges if they were

available. We are also convinced that such
schools could be better able than poorer Negro
colleges to offer a wide range of valuable services to their students. If coordinated with the
state senior colleges, the junior colleges could
substantially benefit by such arrangements as
faculty exchange and shared facilities. Even the
best designed program of improvement for the
poorer Negro colleges would be limited by their
carefully guarded autonomy; their wide variety of
auspices with differing, and frequently con-
flicting, interests; and in many cases, their
very small enrollment.

It is realized, of course, that the public
junior college, if sufficiently mismanaged, could
be as poor a school as the poorest of the predominantly Negro colleges. On the other hand, and
for the reasons advanced above, we feel that
junior colleges could provide a more useful education than the majority of the "poor" four-year
primarily Negro colleges. In any event, the number of public junior colleges is increasing, and
more Negro students are entering them. Since they
are here anyhow, it would be wiser public policy
to have good rather than poor schools.

The two-year public colleges advocated would
chiefly face the problem of the existing, and
probably continuing, educational deficits of the
Negro students who would enter them. On the model
of many of the present public junior colleges,
alternate programs could be developed to meet the
various needs of the students, with strong over-
all emphasis on two years of essentially remedial
work to overcome, to the extent possible, these
educational deficits. Effective counselling would
turn students with as yet unrealized potential to
a transfer program and eventual baccalaureates.
Students with less promise could be directed
toward terminal educational programs in subjects
most useful for obtaining better jobs.

We are not suggesting that two-year public colleges would solve the problem of the Southern Negro high school senior with marked academic deficiencies who aspires, nevertheless, to attend college. The basic problem is that of the academic deficiencies. We simply feel that attendance at integrated colleges with several kinds of programs, where the larger resources of the public educational establishment are available, offers a better prospect than attendance at small segregated institutions with a long history of academic deficiencies.

The High Quality Colleges

The less than two dozen "good" Negro colleges do not present a major problem. Some of them are, in fact, racially integrated to a considerable extent, and apparently most of those that are not would welcome white students if they should apply for admission. For these schools the extent of integration generally follows the extent of overall racial integration in the region in which the school is located. Academically, these schools, if not among the top colleges in the country, are at least relatively sound. Their students, if somewhat below the national academic norm, are far from hopelessly so. Relatively small amounts of money intelligently spent on these "good" colleges should pay large dividends, and we would recommend such selective expenditure.

The Students

The Able College Entrants

We recommend allocation of considerable moneys and effort to the problem of the more able Southern Negro high school seniors who currently enter inferior colleges. The evidence suggests that the brighter students who enter poor colleges

do so chiefly for economic reasons. Better colleges are usually more expensive and often require
that the student move out of state to attend them.
Large increases in financial aid for such students
are a worthwhile expenditure and should be provided.

Apparently over a third of the more able
college entrants enroll in sub-standard schools.
In addition, about half of the more able Southern
Negro high school graduates do not enter college
at all. For these two groups we suggest that
moneys be spent on increased recruitment efforts,
on the part of both the better Negro colleges and
the academically sound primarily white four-year
colleges. Such students should be welcome at both
types of institutions.

More specifically, we feel that the search
for academically promising Negro youth in the high
schools of the South should be centrally organized
far more than it has been in the past and should
be a far more comprehensive effort. In recent
years a number of independent organizations have
developed programs to locate talented Negro youth
in high school and to assist them in entrance to
quality colleges. But these efforts have been
limited by the size of the organizations and the
funding available for such projects. Consequently, efforts have been devoted chiefly to
finding outstanding youth, not simply academically
able Negro youth, and assistance has been offered
to numerically small numbers of students.

For example, the 1964 National Merit Scholarship Corporation's attempt to "call attention to
the most able Negro youth and to help financially
as many to attend college as funds will permit"
assisted a total of 224 students from among 629
finalists and an additional 1,958 students who
were commended and probably were worthy of
scholarship aid. Furthermore, not all high

schools submitted nominations so that there must
be an additional but unknown number of qualified
students who received no aid. The 1965 program
was similar in scope to the one just described.[1]
The finalists, then, represented a small proportion of a large aggregate of able students.

The National Scholarship Service and Fund for
Negro Students has conducted a similar talent
search for some years, but once again assistance
is finally given to a small number of unusually
able students.[2] The initial recruitment literature goes only to students who take scholastic
aptitude tests and, as we found in our study, such
tests are not given in many Southern high schools,
and only to limited numbers of students in many
that do administer them.

The Poorly Prepared College Entrants

As suggested previously, remedial work is
required in an effort to overcome some of the
academic deficiencies. We think that the public
two-year college is one place in which such
training can be given. Some of the four-year primarily Negro colleges also provide such work, but
not enough; the better four-year colleges should
be encouraged and aided to provide more such services.

Pre-College Education

So far we have not spoken of the basic educational problem of Southern Negro youth, but
simply of measures at the college level designed
to ameliorate damage already incurred. The basic
problem, the cumulative educational deficit of the
pre-college student, is not limited to Southern
Negro youth, but includes groups of educationally
deprived youth throughout the country, of whatever
ethnic stock. Southern Negro students simply
represent a particularly disadvantaged minority.

We believe that the preponderance of moneys and
efforts should be expended, over the long term, in
this area.

This problem of a cumulative educational
deficit for specific groups of children cannot be
fully resolved in a year, or a decade, or probably
in several decades. In addition, we do not believe that there is sufficient specific knowledge
about the causes of this deprivation, and their
relative significance, to justify broad escalation
of "action programs" at this time.

Nor can we say with any certainty, in spite
of extensive recent research on this question,
just how significant the quality or content of
teaching is, relative to the socio-economic status
of parents, or to the socio-economic status of the
community in which the child grew up, or the
socio-economic status of the pupil's classmates,
or even innate abilities.[3] For example, the two
most extensive efforts to evaluate the importance
of socio-economic status--the Office of Education's Equality of Educational Opportunity study
and the United States Commission on Civil Rights'
report, Racial Isolation in the Public Schools[4]--
in our opinion largely fail to achieve this objective, though they do succeed in documenting
very well the extent to which the Negro minority
is educationally deprived. We will not attempt an
extended critique of these studies, but will only
indicate by a single example the type of inade-
quacy which we feel casts doubt on many of the
conclusions reached. For both studies the measure
of educational attainment consisted of the test
performance of students. The tests used were ones
which quite specifically are designed to measure
the cumulative impact of a student's total
learning experience, including that which he
learned at home, rather than the effects of the
formal schooling per se. In this context, it is
something of a redundancy to conclude, as these
studies do, that the student's socio-economic

status, and the socio-economic statuses of his classmates, are more educationally significant than the
academic "hardware" and "software" the student
encounters. Other and different tests, ones specifically designed to measure the formal skills
and bodies of fact which schools are primarily
organized to impart, might well have yielded
different results.

Nor have the socio-economic patterns of
school desegregation, as it is in fact occurring,
been precisely evaluated for their effects on educationally deprived groups of students. On this
point we feel that the Civil Rights Commission's
study, which concluded that racial integration in
the nation's schools would be the single most
effective means of decreasing the educational
disadvantage suffered by Negroes, again largely
failed to prove its case. The socio-economic indicator upon which most of the apparent findings
depend, and hence the policy recommendations, is
the educational level of the student's parents.
Negro and white students with parents educated at
the same level belong to different socio-economic
classes by virtue of the fact that, at the same
educational levels, white persons earn considerably
more than do nonwhites.[5] The apparent advantage
for Negroes in attending schools with large proportions of white children, controlling for the
level of parental education at the school, could
simply be the benefits accruing from attendance
with financially more affluent schoolmates, and
their correlates. One correlate, for example, is
simply a more prosperous school district which can
afford to, and does, spend more on public education.

Integration per se, as it is in fact
occurring, and is likely to occur in the future,
might have little positive effect, or even a
negative effect, upon the academic level of performance of pupils of a racial minority. Here
again we feel that further evidence is needed, and

research with far more adequate controls of the
relevant factors. To date, integration of schools
generally seems to have placed relatively low
socio-economic children of both racial groups in
the same classrooms. Unless the pattern were to
be radically altered in the future, the educational benefits would seem far from certain.

In brief, we feel that the initial task is to
assemble the scattered, though extensive, data on
causes of educational deprivation; some assembly
work is now under way, but not nearly enough.[6]
The second task is to review the evidence,
initiate new research where information is
lacking, or conclusions are unclear or not sufficiently explicit, and then to design remedial
policies and programs based on the final conclusions as to causes and their relative weights.
Once initiated, such a project would take perhaps
a decade, or even more, to complete. It would require the assurance of considerable moneys during
the entire span, and would logically be the re-
sponsibility of the Federal Office of Education.
It would enlist the assistance of principal universities and other private groups engaged in educational research, and the approach should be
cross-disciplinary. In the past the findings of
psychologists, anthropologists, geneticists,
sociologists, and professional educators have all
too often stemmed from research designed within
the limited perspectives and concerns of a particular discipline.

We are not suggesting that current efforts to
improve the schooling of educationally deprived
children should cease, but simply that there
should be no great escalation of these efforts
until we have a clearer knowledge of the likely
"returns" on investment. Indeed, political and
other pressures are almost certain to increase expenditures on "action programs" in the foreseeable
future, whether or not the research we suggest is
undertaken. Accordingly, we stress here the need

for continuing large-scale basic research, since
this aspect will be omitted from any politically
inspired action program, whether instigated by a
government unit or a private foundation.

We cannot carry our recommendations beyond
this initial suggestion for over-all assessment,
since the assessment would determine where subsequent moneys and efforts should be expended. But
we do feel that such assessment is imperative.

NOTES TO CHAPTER 10

1. Tenth Annual Review of Research, Vol. 2,
No. 11 (Evanston, Ill.: National Merit Scholarship
Corporation, 1966), p. 2.

Warren S. Blumenfeld, Some Characteristics of
Finalists in the 1966 National Achievement
Scholarship Program, NMSC Research Reports, Vol.
2, No. 4 (Evanston, Ill.: National Merit Scholarship Corporation, 1966).

Roy J. Roberts and Robert C. Nichols, Participants in the National Achievement Scholarship
Program for Negroes, NMSC Research Reports, Vol.
2, No. 2 (Evanston, Ill.: National Merit Scholarship Corporation, 1966).

2. Kenneth B. Clark and Laurence Plotkin,
The Negro Student at Integrated Colleges (New
York: National Scholarship Service and Fund for
Negro Students, 1963), p. 12.

3. After more than a half century of research and controversy on the "sensitive" topic of
possible genetically based differences in learning
potential, no clear answers have emerged, despite
assertions to the contrary by experts who reach
differing conclusions on identical evidence;
nevertheless, considerable progress in achieving

a better educated population can be made by con-
centrating on the social, economic, and cultural
variables.

4.   James S. Coleman, et al., Equality of
Educational Opportunity (Washington, D.C.: U.S.
Office of Education, 1966); and Racial Isolation
in the Public Schools, Vol. 1, A Report of the
U.S. Commission on Civil Rights (Washington,
D.C.: U.S. Government Printing Office, 1967).

5.   For example, in 1959 the median income of
men having completed four years or more of college
was about $7,800 for whites and $4,800 for nonwhites (U.S. Bureau of the Census. U.S. Census of
Population: 1960. Detailed Characteristics, U.S.
Summary (Final Report PC(1)-1D; Washington, D.C.:
U.S. Government Printing Office, 1963). For men
who only finished high school median income was
about $5,500 for whites and $3,700 for nonwhites.

6.   See: Edmund W. Gordon and Doxey A.
Wilkerson, Compensatory Education for the Disad-
vantaged (New York: College Entrance Examination
Board, 1966).

APPENDIX   A

STATISTICAL TABLES

APPENDIX A STATISTICAL
TABLES

NOTES ON THE DATA AND THE TABULATIONS

The tables in this appendix may be divided
into four groups, as follows:

Group 1. Tables 1 through 8, documenting information received
from officials at the four-
year primarily Negro col-
leges. Topics include trends
in enrollment, recruitment,
admissions practices and
preferences, and student
financial aid.

Group 2. Tables 9 through 13, documenting information received
from Southern Negro high
schools regarding their
Spring, 1965, seniors
planning on entering college
the following Fall.

Group 3. Tables 14 through 31, deriving
from responses to our survey
of Fall, 1965, students enrolled in the primarily Negro
colleges of various types and
qualities.

143

Group 4.   Tables 32 through 34, representing supplementary data
which we did not gather our-
selves in the course of our
study, but which are basic
to important sections of our
analysis.

The tables in Group 3 require some prefatory
and explanatory remarks.

First, the tabulations include a small number
of students (ninety) at three Southern integrated
colleges. The analysis makes little comment on
this small sample, and we do not lay claim to its
representativeness.

The analytic categories for each table are
identical, save that a few tables include comparisons of college population groups with larger
population groups. For example, the occupational
distribution of fathers of various groups of college students are compared with this same occupational distribution for all Southern nonwhite
males.

Each table presents two sets of analytic
categories. The first set consists of a total of
seventy-one colleges divided into six groups,
representing different types of colleges in terms
of auspice, length of academic program, geographical location, integration status and, for four-
year Negro colleges, accreditation status.

In the second set of forty-three colleges,
the four-year Southern accredited primarily Negro
colleges in our sample are divided into three
tabulation groups, determined by the quality
ratings accorded each college "by six cognoscenti
of predominantly Negro colleges." Excluded from
this second set of tabulations are the three integrated primarily white Southern colleges. Also

excluded are the two-year colleges, not rated as
to quality, and which, moreover, differ widely
from senior colleges in their academic program
and educational objectives.

The two Northern primarily Negro colleges are
both rated high on the quality index. On the
other hand, 8 out of 9 four-year nonaccredited
colleges are rated in the lowest of the three
categories used in our tabulations and the ninth
barely qualifies for the "fair" rating group.
Since the Northern colleges and the nonaccredited
four-year colleges are separately tabulated in the
first set of tables for type of college, and since
both groups are relatively uniform as to quality,
there was nothing additional to learn by including
them in these "quality" tabulations. Accordingly,
they are excluded. One four-year accredited college was a two-year school at the time of rating,
and so was not rated. The 131 respondents from
this college represent only 2 per cent of all
respondents in four-year accredited colleges in
our sample, and their absence from the second set
of tabulations is consequently of minor significance.

The two sets of tabulations may each be considered in several ways--as simple descriptive
marginals for each of the college-type sub-samples,
or each of the college-quality groups--or else as
cross-tabulations in which the various sub-samples
are compared for the distributions of the student
variables. Furthermore, it is possible to ask,
for the four-year accredited colleges, whether it
is the quality of the college or its type (in this
instance whether public or private) that is most
related to large differences in student characteristics.

Table 1

Quality, type, and location of college by changes
in total enrollment, 1962, 1965, and
expected for 1968

Changes in Total Enrollment

	1962-1965	1965-1968	1962-1968
	%	%	%
Public colleges (4-year):	27	21	54
"Poor"	33	27	70
"Fair"	31	20	57
"Good"	15	17	34
Private colleges (4-year):	20	26	51
"Poor"	16	40	62
"Fair"	23	26	56
"Good"	17	18	38
Public and private colleges (4-year)	23	23	52
"Poor"	27	32	67
"Fair"	27	23	56
"Good"	16	17	36
Colleges located* in:			
"Deep South"	25	21	52
"Other South"	18	23	44
Border states	30	28	66
Ohio and Pennsylvania	54	37	111
All colleges	23	24	53

*Deep South - Alabama, Arkansas, Georgia, Mississippi, South Carolina.
Other South - Florida, Louisiana, North Carolina, Tennessee, Texas,
        Virginia.
Border states - Delaware, District of Columbia, Kentucky, Maryland,
        Missouri, Oklahoma, West Virginia.

146

Table 2

Per cent increase in new entrants, 1962-1965,
by quality of college and location of college

	All colleges	Poor colleges	Fair colleges	Good colleges
	%	%	%	%
"Deep South"	34	47	37	3
"Other South" and border states	18	30	13	21
Total	25	43	20	18
No. of colleges	70	27	25	18

Table 3

Quality of college by per cent increases in new applicants,
applicants accepted, and acceptances in fact
entering colleges, 1962-1965

	All colleges	"Poor" colleges	"Fair" colleges	"Good" colleges
	%	%	%	%
Per cent increase in applicants, 1962-1965	23	56	13	16
Per cent increase in acceptances, 1962-1965	14	39	2	16
Per cent increase in actual new entrants, 1962-1965	25	43	20	18

Quality of college by applicant-acceptance rate,
and acceptance-entrant rate, 1962 and 1965

	All colleges	"Poor" colleges	"Fair" colleges	"Good" colleges
Applicant-acceptance rate				
1962	.76	.78	.80	.68
1965	.70	.69	.72	.68
Change 1962-1965	-.06	-.09	-.08	±.00
Acceptance-entrant rate				
1962	.71	.80	.66	.72
1965	.78	.82	.78	.74
Change 1962-1965	+.07	+.02	+.12	+.02

Table 4

Quality of college by proportions of colleges
which have a full-time recruitment person
or a person for whom recruitment is an
important part of the official job

Presence or not of recruitment person	All colleges	"Poor" colleges	"Fair" colleges	"Good" colleges
	%	%	%	%
Yes	85	90	85	95
Full-time	18	4	31	28
Important part of job	67	86	54	67
No	15	10	15	5
All responses	100	100	100	100

Table 5

Quality of college by reasons given for expansion
of recruitment program in the next three years

Reason for expansion	All colleges	"Poor" colleges	"Fair" colleges	"Good" colleges
To get high quality students, or to meet increased competition for better students	25	7	14	4
Simply an effect of growth of the college	13	4	6	3
Increased demand for college or increase in college-age population	7	3	3	1
More government monies for recruitment and/or expansion expected	4	3	1	-
To provide a more balanced enrollment-- or a more diversified enrollment--white students, able Negro students from integrated high schools, geographically diverse students, etc.	9	2	2	5
Simply to increase enrollment	3	-	1	2
To attract local or in-state students, commuting students	2	1	-	1
To get able, but deprived, students	2	-	2	-
All other reasons	3	2	-	1
All reasons	68	22	29	17

NOTE: We have tabulated simply the number of mentions of particular
reasons since the number of responses appears too few to warrant
percentaging. Some colleges gave more than one reason.

Table 6

Proportions of colleges of different qualities especially anxious
to enroll particular types or groups of students

Types or groups of students	All colleges	"Poor" colleges	"Fair" colleges	"Good" colleges
	%	%	%	%
Students with unusual academic potential	84	82	82	94
Students with unusually good secondary school records	83	86	86	88
Other than Negro students	53	46	61	69
Students from the state in which the college is located	52	71	46	25
Students from socially or economically deprived backgrounds	51	43	36	69
Students from other parts of the country	47	43	50	56
Students from the community where the college is located, or its immediate vicinity	44	46	36	37
Students especially well qualified in particular academic areas	35	36	36	25
Athletes	32	43	18	12
Out-of-state Southern students	22	25	25	19
Foreign students	21	11	36	12
Students with particular vocational objectives	16	11	14	31

Table 7

Quality of college by the one most important criterion
for the student admission decision

The one most important criterion	All colleges	"Poor" colleges	"Fair" colleges	"Good" colleges
	%	%	%	%
The student's high school record	58	52	63	71
Student test-score data	8	6	11	10
That the student is an accredited or approved high school graduate	11	10	11	10
That the student simply has graduated from high school	9	20	8	--
Student's expressed desire for a college education	6	6	--	--
All other criteria	8	6	7	9
All criteria	100	100	100	100

Table 8

Quality of college by proportions of students
receiving financial aid of various kinds

Type of financial aid	All colleges	"Poor" colleges	"Fair" colleges	"Good" colleges
	%	%	%	%
Scholarship aid from college	21	20	17	28
Federal work-study program	15	16	12	18
Federal loan program	23	33	20	19

Table 9

Type and location of college entered by location of high school
from which graduated in Spring, 1965

	Location of high school								
	Total			With test scores			No test scores		
Type of college	Total	Deep South	Other South	Total	Deep South	Other South	Total	Deep South	Other South
TOTAL	100.0	100.0	100.0	100.0	100.0	100.0	100.0	100.0	100.0
Negro colleges	78.0	83.8	73.5	80.4	85.1	77.2	71.8	81.0	62.7
4-year	73.3	75.6	71.6	76.7	79.0	75.0	65.1	68.8	61.5
"Good"	25.7	14.5	34.2	28.5	16.4	36.8	18.7	10.7	26.6
"Fair"	32.6	40.3	26.7	33.1	41.2	27.5	31.5	38.6	24.6
"Poor"	15.0	20.8	10.7	15.1	21.4	10.7	14.9	19.5	10.3
2-year private	4.6	8.2	1.9	3.7	6.1	2.1	6.7	12.2	1.2
Integrated colleges	22.0	16.2	26.5	19.6	14.9	22.8	28.2	19.0	37.3
In South	19.0	12.6	24.0	16.3	10.8	20.0	25.9	16.3	35.5
4-year	8.4	6.0	10.3	8.4	7.2	9.3	8.4	3.6	13.2
2-year	10.6	6.6	13.7	7.9	3.6	10.7	17.5	12.7	22.3
In North and West	3.0	3.6	2.5	3.3	4.1	2.8	2.3	2.7	1.8
4-year	2.1	2.7	1.7	2.3	3.2	1.7	1.6	1.7	1.5
2 year	0.9	0.9	0.8	1.0	0.9	1.1	0.7	1.0	0.3
Number of cases	4,129	1,791	2,338	2,942	1,202	1,740	1,187	589	598

154

Table 10

Test-score ranking of students by location of high school
and type and location of college entered

Location of high school from which graduated

Type of college entered	Total			"Deep South"			"Other South"		
	Total	Top half	Bottom half	Total	Top half	Bottom half	Total	Top half	Bottom half
	%	%	%	%	%	%	%	%	%
Negro colleges	80.4	70.0	83.9	85.1	66.9	90.2	77.2	71.6	79.2
4-year	76.6	68.0	79.5	78.9	65.8	82.6	75.1	69.2	77.2
"Good"	28.5	32.6	27.2	16.4	25.1	14.0	36.8	36.8	36.9
"Fair"	33.0	29.5	34.2	41.2	34.2	43.1	27.5	26.8	27.7
"Poor"	15.1	5.9	18.1	21.3	6.5	25.5	10.8	5.6	12.6
2-year private	3.8	2.0	4.4	6.2	1.1	7.6	2.1	2.4	2.0
Integrated colleges	19.6	30.0	16.1	14.9	33.1	9.8	22.8	28.4	20.8
In South	16.3	21.9	14.4	10.8	22.1	7.7	20.1	21.9	19.4
4-year	8.4	18.3	5.2	7.1	20.2	3.5	9.3	17.3	6.4
2-year	7.9	3.6	9.2	3.7	1.9	4.2	10.8	4.5	13.0
In North and West	3.3	8.1	1.7	4.1	11.0	2.1	2.7	6.5	1.4
4-year	2.3	6.9	0.8	3.2	10.2	1.2	1.7	5.0	0.5
2-year	1.0	1.2	0.9	0.9	0.8	0.9	1.0	1.5	0.9
All colleges	100.0	100.0	100.0	100.0	100.0	100.0	100.0	100.0	100.0
Number of cases	2,942	725	2,217	1,202	263	939	1,740	462	1,278

155

Table 11

Number in high school graduating class, by location of high school,
by per cent distribution of test-score ranking of students

Location of high school and test-score rank of student	Number in graduating class			
	Under 50	50 to 90	100 and over	Total
"Deep South"				
Test-score rank	100	100	100	100
Top half	14	9	31	22
Bottom half	86	91	69	78
No. of cases	247	324	664	1,235
"Other South"				
Test-score rank	100	100	100	100
Top half	21	28	28	26
Bottom half	79	72	72	74
No. of cases	377	575	815	1,767
Total South				
Test-score rank	100	100	100	100
Top half	18	21	29	24
Bottom half	82	79	71	76
No. of cases	624	899	1,479	3,002

Table 12

Number of college entrants by location of high school
by per cent distribution of test-score ranking
of students

Location of high school and test-score rank of student	Number of college entrants from high school			
	Under 25	25 to 99	100 and over	Total
"Deep South"				
Test-score rank	100	100	100	100
Top half	13	21	44	22
Bottom half	87	79	56	78
No. of cases	480	541	214	1,235
"Other South"				
Test-score rank	100	100	100	100
Top half	23	27	37	26
Bottom half	77	73	63	74
No. of cases	828	732	207	1,767
Total South				
Test-score rank	100	100	100	100
Top half	19	24	41	24
Bottom half	81	76	59	76
No. of cases	1,308	1,273	421	3,002

Table 13

Per cent distribution of size of college entered, by location
of high school and test-score ranking of students

Size of college (number of students)	Total			"Deep South"			"Other South"		
		Test score			Test score			Test score	
	Total	Top half	Bottom half	Total	Top half	Bottom half	Total	Top half	Bottom half
TOTAL	100	100	100	100	100	100	100	100	100
Under 500	12	5	14	15	4	19	9	6	10
500 to 1,499	40	36	41	53	46	55	30	29	30
1,500 to 2,999	19	23	18	20	22	20	19	24	17
3,000 to 9,999	26	29	25	10	23	5	38	33	41
10,000 and over	3	7	2	2	5	1	4	8	2
No. of cases	2,962	726	2,236	1,219	266	953	1,743	460	1,283

Table 14

Occupational distribution of Southern nonwhite males,[a] and of the fathers of students, by type and quality of college

Major occupational group	Southern non-white males	Type						Quality		
		Two Northern 4-year	4-year Southern				2-year Southern	4-year accredited		
			Accredited		Non-accredited	"Integrated"		"Good"	"Fair"	"Poor"
			Public	Private						
TOTAL	100	100	100	100	100	100	100	100	100	100
White-collar	9	41	20	34	15	18	13	34	27	18
Upper	5	32	16	27	12	17	10	27	21	14
Prof. and technical	3	18	12	20	9	12	7	19	16	11
Mgrs., officials and proprietors (exc. farm)	2	14	4	7	3	5	3	8	5	3
Lower	4	9	4	7	3	1	3	7	6	4
Manual (exc. farm)	70	51	61	57	68	64	55	59	58	61
Farm	21	8	19	9	17	18	32	7	15	21

[a] Male heads of households, 35 to 64 years of age, with own children under age 25, 1960 (Source: U.S. Census of Population, 1960, Families, PC(2)4A, Table 12).

Table 15

Labor force status and occupational distribution for the mothers of students,
by type and quality of college

Labor force status and major occupational group	Type						Quality		
	Two Northern 4-year	4-year Southern				2-year Southern	4-year accredited		
		Accredited		Non-accredited	"Integrated"		"Good"	"Fair"	"Poor"
		Public	Private						
LABOR FORCE STATUS	100	100	100	100	100	100	100	100	100
in labor force	47	48	56	43	43	40	57	52	49
Not in labor force	53	52	44	57	57	60	43	48	51
MAJOR OCCUPATIONAL GROUP	100	100	100	100	100	100	100	100	100
White-collar	55	38	51	28	27	22	54	45	32
Upper	32	29	41	23	22	17	43	35	27
Prof. and technical	30	27	38	23	17	14	39	32	24
Mgrs., officials and proprietors (exc. farm)	2	2	3	--	5	3	4	3	3
Lower	23	9	10	5	5	5	11	10	5
Manual (exc. farm)	45	60	48	67	73	70	45	53	64
Farm	--	2	1	5	--	8	1	2	4

Table 16

Years of schooling completed for Southern nonwhite males,[a] and for the fathers of students, by type and quality of college

Years of schooling	Southern non-white males	Two Northern 4-year	Type					Quality		
			4-year Southern					4-year accredited		
			Accredited		Non-accredited	"Integrated"	2-year Southern	"Good"	"Fair"	"Poor"
			Public	Private						
TOTAL	100	100	100	100	100	100	100	100	100	100
1 – 8 years	78	20	37	27	35	35	42	27	32	37
1 – 7 years	68	11	17	13	16	14	21	13	15	17
8 years	10	9	20	14	19	21	21	14	17	20
9 or more years	22	80	63	73	65	65	58	73	68	63
9 – 11 years	12	21	28	23	32	23	34	22	26	29
12 years[b]	6	31	21	24	22	26	15	25	23	19
13 – 15 years	2	10	6	9	5	9	5	9	8	6
16 years	1	10	5	9	4	6	3	8	6	6
16 or more years	1	8	3	8	2	1	1	9	5	3
Median years of schooling	5.1	11.3	9.4	11.0	9.4	10.0	8.7	12.0	11.1	9.3

[a] Males 35-64 years of age (Source: U.S. Census of Population, Educational Attainment, PC(2)5B, Table 2).

[b] Includes a very small proportion of men who had some post-high school technical training, but no college work.

161

Table 17

Years of schooling completed for Southern nonwhite females,[a] and for the mothers of students, by type and quality of college

Years of schooling	Southern non-white females	Two Northern 4-year	Type 4-year Southern Accredited Public	Accredited Private	Non-accredited	"Integrated"	2-year Southern	Quality 4-year accredited "Good"	"Fair"	"Poor"
TOTAL	100	100	100	100	100	100	100	100	100	100
1 – 8 years	71	13	22	17	22	27	31	16	19	24
1 – 7 years	58	7	8	6	7	12	10	6	7	8
8 years	13	6	14	11	15	15	21	10	12	16
9 or more years	29	87	78	83	78	73	69	84	81	76
9 – 11 years	15	21	33	25	38	21	41	24	30	34
12 years[b]	8	37	27	28	25	40	17	29	28	25
13 – 15 years	3	15	7	10	8	7	6	9	9	7
16 years	2	8	9	13	5	3	4	15	10	8
16 or more years	1	6	2	7	2	2	1	7	4	2
Median years of schooling	6.0	11.5	10.5	11.3	10.2	11.1	9.4	11.4	11.0	10.3

[a] Females 35–64 years of age (Source: U.S. Census of Population, Educational Attainment, PC(2)5B, Table 2).

[b] Includes a very small proportion of women who had some post-high school technical training, but no college work.

162

Table 18

Income distribution for Southern nonwhite families,[a] and for the student's immediate household, by type and quality of college

Annual family income	Southern non-white households	Two Northern 4-year	Type 4-year Southern Accredited Public	Private	Non-accredited	"Integrated"	2-year Southern	Quality 4-year accredited "Good"	"Fair"	"Poor"
TOTAL	100	100	100	100	100	100	100	100	100	100
Under $4,000	67	20	53	41	64	42	75	33	49	60
Under $2,000	32	3	21	12	26	19	34	9	16	27
$2,000-2,999	19	7	16	14	21	11	23	11	16	18
$3,000-3,999	16	10	16	15	17	12	18	13	17	15
$4,000-9,999	29	53	41	45	34	55	23	54	40	36
$4,000-4,999	11	9	13	13	12	23	11	13	11	15
$5,000-5,999	6	12	10	11	9	19	6	13	10	8
$6,000-7,999	7	22	11	13	10	8	4	17	12	8
$8,000-9,999	5	10	7	8	3	5	2	11	7	5
$10,000 and over	4	27	6	14	2	3	2	13	11	4
Median income	$2,898	$6,820	$3,813	$4,692	$3,176	$4,348	$2,696	$5,308	$4,091	$3,303

[a]Source: Current Population Reports, Consumer Income, Series P-60, No. 47, September 1965, Table 13, p. 33.

163

Table 19

Family income distribution for students in primarily Negro colleges,
and for all U. S. college students

Annual family income	Our sample, 1966	Institute of Higher Education sample, 1963[a]	All college students, 1960[b]
TOTAL	100	100	100
Under $4,000	51	42	8
$4,000-5,999	22	26	14
$6,000-9,999	18	22	37
$10,000 and over	9	10	41
Number of students	5,826	6,323	--
Number of colleges	68	89	--
Median income	$3,921	$4,626	$8,064

[a] Earl J. McGrath, The Predominantly Negro Colleges in Transition,
Institute of Higher Education, Teachers College, Columbia University,
New York, 1965, Table 8, p. 39.

[b] An estimate from Rexford G. Moon, Jr., "A Model for Determining
Future Student Aid Needs in the United States for the Support of
Full-Time Undergraduate Education," duplicated, 1964, Table 5,
p. 12.

Table 20

Distribution by location of high school from which student graduated, by type and quality of college

Location of high school	Type						Quality		
	Two Northern 4-year	4-year Southern				2-year Southern	4-year accredited		
		Accredited		Non-accredited	"integrated"		"Good"	"Fair"	"Poor"
		Public	Private						
TOTAL	100	100	100	100	100	100	100	100	100
Southern states (under 8% Negroes in school with white children)	6	77	80	98	51	99	72	79	86
Under 1%	5	35	38	71	1	55	29	35	48
1.1 - 7.9%	1	42	42	27	50	44	43	44	38
Border states (over 30% Negroes in school with white children)	10	16	5	--	47	--	13	11	8
All other continental U.S.	73	7	13	2	2	1	14	9	6
Outside continental U.S.	11	--	2	--	--	--	1	1	--

165

Table 21

Location of college by location of high school from which student graduated, by type and quality of college

Location of high school and college	Two Northern 4-year	Type					Quality		
		4-year Southern				2-year Southern	4-year accredited		
		Accredited Public	Accredited Private	Non-accredited	"Integrated"		"Good"	"Fair"	"Poor"
TOTAL	100	100	100	100	100	100	100	100	100
Same community or county	7	16	21	40	33	42	22	19	16
Same state – other county	25	67	36	51	64	52	35	55	65
Same region – other state	20	10	27	8	2	5	28	17	13
Different regions	37	7	14	1	1	1	14	8	6
High school out of U.S.	11	--	2	--	--	--	1	1	--

Table 22

Desired region of residence after finishing college, by type and quality of college

Desired region of future residence	Type						Quality		
	Two Northern 4-year	4-year Southern				2-year Southern	4-year accredited		
		Accredited		Non-accredited	"Integrated"		"Good"	"Fair"	"Poor"
		Public	Private						
TOTAL	100	100	100	100	100	100	100	100	100
The Western or Mountain states	12	19	18	18	34	24	19	18	19
The North Central states	16	24	18	26	10	26	17	23	24
The Northeastern or Middle Atlantic states	51	28	26	12	19	11	32	25	21
Outside the continental U.S.	16	3	3	2	2	3	3	3	2
The Southern or South Central states	5	27	35	42	35	36	29	31	34

Table 23

Distribution by major field of study, by type and quality of college

Major Field of Study	Two Northern 4-year	Type					Quality		
		4-year Southern				2-year Southern	4-year accredited		
		Accredited Public	Accredited Private	Non-accredited	"Integrated"		"Good"	"Fair"	"Poor"
TOTAL	100	100	100	100	100	100	100	100	100
Natural and physical sciences	19	15	22	16	18	14	25	18	14
Agriculture	--	2	--	--	--	1	1	2	1
Biology and biol. sciences	12	6	10	8	6	6	11	7	7
Mathematical subjects	3	5	7	7	4	4	8	6	4
All other[a]	4	2	5	1	8	3	5	3	2
Social and life sciences	37	17	24	23	14	13	23	21	17
Sociology and social studies	11	8	11	5	7	3	10	11	6
History	6	3	4	9	3	3	4	4	4
Political science and government	8	1	3	1	2	1	4	--	--
Psychology	9	1	4	--	1	--	4	2	1
All other	3	4	2	8	1	6	1	4	6
Education	18	40	22	36	30	35	23	27	46
Elementary education	10	22	14	20	18	15	14	15	27
Business education	1	7	3	9	4	8	3	4	8
Physical education	1	8	3	6	4	9	4	5	9
All other	6	3	2	1	4	3	2	3	2

[a] Includes medical and "other" technology

168

	Type						Quality		
	Two Northern 4-year	4-year Southern				2-year Southern	4-year accredited		
		Accredited		Non-accredited	"Integrated"		"Good"	"Fair"	"Poor"
Major field of study		Public	Private						
Business and commerce	12	7	9	10	14	15	8	10	5
Business administration	8	4	5	5	5	4	5	6	3
All other	4	3	4	5	9	11	3	4	2
Humanities	7	10	14	13	7	8	11	12	12
English and foreign languages and literature	4	6	10	9	4	4	8	8	10
Music, fine arts, and speech	3	3	3	4	3	4	3	4	2
Philosophy, theology, and religion	--	--	1	--	--	--	--	--	--
Social and health services	4	7	5	2	7	7	6	7	5
Home economics	1	4	2	2	5	4	3	3	4
Social work and administration, and guidance	2	1	1	--	--	--	1	2	--
Nursing and health professions n.e.c.	1	2	2	--	2	3	2	2	1
Technical arts and sciences	3	1	3	--	8	6	4	4	1
Engineering	3	1	2	--	2	1	2	2	--
Architecture, design, indus. arts, and allied	--	2	1	--	6	2	1	1	1
Trade and industrial training[b]	--	1	--	--	--	3	1	1	--
All other majors	--	--	1	--	2	2	--	1	--

[b] Vocational

Table 24

Selected scholastic characteristics of students,
by type and quality of college

Scholastic characteristics	Type						Quality		
	Two Northern 4-year	4-year Southern				2-year Southern	4-year accredited		
		Accredited		Non-accredited	"Integrated"		"Good"	"Fair"	"Poor"
		Public	Private						
	%	%	%	%	%	%	%	%	%
Degree-credit student	94	92	92	86	87	81	94	92	89
Full-time student	99	99	98	98	98	96	98	99	99
Took a college preparatory course in high school	80	77	82	76	88	74	82	80	78
Plans to attend graduate or professional school	82	78	83	78	82	79	82	81	80

Table 25

Expected major occupational group after finishing college, by type and quality of college

Expected major occupational group	Type						Quality		
	Two Northern 4-year	4-year Southern				2-year Southern	4-year accredited		
		Accredited		Non-accredited	"Integrated"		"Good"	"Fair"	"Poor"
		Public	Private						
TOTAL	100	100	100	100	100	100	100	100	100
White-collar	100	98	100	99	100	96	100	100	99
Upper	97	94	96	89	92	82	97	95	94
Prof. and technical	92	92	93	87	89	80	94	92	93
Mgrs., officials, and proprietors	5	2	3	2	3	2	3	3	1
Lower	3	4	4	10	8	14	3	5	5
Manual (exc. farm)	--	1	--	1	--	4	--	--	1
Farm	--	--	--	--	--	--	--	--	--
Armed Forces	--	1	--	--	--	--	--	--	--

Table 26

Expected specific occupations for students who intend to be
professional workers, by type and quality of college

Expected occupation	Two Northern 4-year	Type					Quality		
		4-year Southern				2-year Southern	4-year accredited		
		Accredited		Non-accredited	"Integrated"		"Good"	"Fair"	"Poor"
		Public	Private						
TOTAL	100	100	100	100	100	100	100	100	100
Teaching	30	62	44	66	54	62	41	53	67
Secondary school	11	21	16	23	17	18	15	19	22
Elementary school	10	21	13	16	19	14	12	16	25
College	7	14	10	20	17	23	9	12	15
Unspecified	2	6	5	7	1	7	5	6	5
Social welfare, group, and recreation work	13	10	12	9	5	5	10	13	8
Therapists (exc. prof. nurses)a	11	4	9	1	1	2	10	5	5
Artists and musicians	2	4	3	6	3	4	4	3	3
Natural scientists	4	2	4	2	--	2	4	3	2
Accountants	5	2	3	2	4	2	4	3	1
Technicians	--	2	2	3	8	3	2	2	2
Social scientists	7	2	4	1	4	1	6	3	1
Professional nurses	2	1	3	1	3	5	2	2	1
Engineers	4	2	2	--	4	2	3	2	1
Dieticians and nutritionists	--	1	1	--	4	1	1	1	1
All other	22	8	13	9	10	11	13	10	8

Table 27

Distribution of students by standing in high school class, by type and quality of college

High school standing	Type						Quality		
	Two Northern 4-year	4-year Southern				2-year Southern	4-year accredited		
		Accredited		Non-accredited	"Inte-grated"		"Good"	"Fair"	"Poor"
		Public	Private						
TOTAL	100	10C	100	100	100	100	100	100	100
Top quarter	40	58	66	46	62	30	70	61	57
Second quarter	39	34	27	43	35	52	24	31	35
Third or bottom quarter	21	8	7	11	3	18	6	8	8

173

Table 28

Number and sources of student financing, by type and quality of college

Financing	Two Northern 4-year	Type 4-year Southern Accredited Public	Accredited Private	Non-accredited	"Integrated"	2-year Southern	Quality 4-year accredited "Good"	"Fair"	"Poor"
TOTAL	100	100	100	100	100	100	100	100	100
One or two sources	59	72	65	77	70	75	66	69	73
One source	34	45	40	51	56	46	42	43	48
Two sources	25	27	25	26	14	29	24	26	25
Three or more sources	41	28	35	23	30	25	34	31	27
Three sources	24	19	21	16	17	17	20	20	19
Four sources	11	8	11	6	10	7	10	9	7
Five or six sources	6	1	3	1	3	1	4	2	1
	%	%	%	%	%	%	%	%	%
Immediate family	66	65	67	59	68	53	69	67	62
Scholarships or other college aid	37	22	32	26	16	22	29	27	25
Government loan or other government aid	30	23	29	36	21	25	26	26	25
Aid from noncollege group	11	5	6	3	4	3	6	6	6
Personal savings	25	17	16	12	17	20	16	17	16
Work during school year	17	18	24	17	28	25	23	21	17
Summer work	41	39	36	27	38	38	36	38	37
Other sources	1	3	3	1	2	1	4	3	3

...sum of funds... percentages add to substantially more than 100% because of multiple mentions.

Table 29

Sex, age, and marital status of students, by type and quality of college

Characteristic	Two Northern 4-year	Type — 4-year Southern Accredited Public	Accredited Private	Non-accredited	"Integrated"	2-year Southern	Quality — 4-year accredited "Good"	"Fair"	"Poor"
SEX	100	100	100	100	100	100	100	100	100
Male	63	38	39	37	42	39	40	40	34
Female	37	62	61	63	59	61	60	60	66
AGE	100	100	100	100	100	100	100	100	100
18 years or less	53	37	48	47	41	46	50	40	38
19 years	21	22	18	17	26	27	19	19	23
20 years	11	15	13	13	13	15	12	15	15
21 years	3	12	11	10	9	6	10	13	11
22 years	1	7	4	5	6	2	4	6	6
23 or 24 years	5	4	2	4	4	1	2	3	3
25 - 29 years	3	2	2	2	1	2	2	3	2
30 years and over	3	1	2	2	--	1	1	1	2
MARITAL STATUS	100	100	100	100	100	100	100	100	100
Never married	95	92	94	93	88	94	95	92	92
Married, living with spouse	3	6	4	6	6	5	4	6	6
Other	2	2	2	1	6	1	1	2	2

Table 30

Year in college and residence arrangements of students, by type and quality of college

| | Type | | | | | | Quality | | |
Characteristic	Two Northern 4-year	4-year Southern Accredited Public	4-year Southern Accredited Private	Non-accredited	"Integrated"	2-year Southern	4-year accredited "Good"	4-year accredited "Fair"	4-year accredited "Poor"
YEAR IN COLLEGE	100	100	100	100	100	100	100	100	100
Freshman	80	42	54	63	49	66	51	45	48
Sophomore	12	23	18	14	23	34	21	20	20
Junior	6	18	14	12	19	--	15	18	16
Senior	2	17	14	11	9	--	13	17	16
TYPE OF RESIDENCE	100	100	100	100	100	100	100	100	100
Student lives in:									
Dormitory or other college residence	91	74	68	49	27	33	73	67	74
Apartment hotel, rooming house, etc.	2	6	7	5	13	14	4	9	6
At home with family	7	16	20	40	57	46	20	19	16
With other relatives or friends	--	4	5	6	3	7	3	5	4

Table 31

Number and sources of encouragement to students to enter college,
by type and quality of college

Encouragement	Two Northern 4-year	4-year Southern				2-year Southern	Quality		
		Accredited		Non-accredited	"Integrated"		4-year accredited		
		Public	Private				"Good"	"Fair"	"Poor"
NUMBER	100	100	100	100	100	100	100	100	100
No one in particular	34	34	34	30	39	27	37	32	33
One person	55	56	53	59	52	62	52	57	54
Two persons	9	8	10	8	3	8	8	8	10
Three persons	2	1	2	2	2	2	2	2	2
Four or more persons	--	1	1	1	4	1	1	1	1
SOURCES OF ENCOURAGEMENT	%	%	%	%	%	%	%	%	%
Mother	36	41	41	46	40	47	38	41	43
Father	19	15	19	15	11	14	19	17	15
Other relative	5	6	6	5	10	6	5	6	6
High school teacher	4	11	8	11	12	10	8	10	10
High school principal	2	3	2	3	4	5	1	3	3
Minister or other church person	7	1	3	2	1	1	1	2	2
Prominent community figure	3	2	1	1	--	2	1	1	2
Other persons	4	3	4	2	2	2	3	3	4

Table 32

Rates* of out-migration from the South,
nonwhites, by age, sex, and education,
1955-1960

| | | Years of schooling | | | | |
	Total	0-8	9-11	12	13-15	16+
MALE						
25-29 years	10.0	5.8	10.7	15.2	18.0	21.7
30-34 years	6.0	4.1	7.8	8.1	11.1	16.7
35-39 years	4.1	3.2	5.2	5.9	7.9	9.3
40-44 years	2.8	2.3	3.4	4.1	4.3	5.1
FEMALE						
25-29 years	8.4	4.6	8.5	11.2	15.9	15.0
30-34 years	4.9	3.5	5.2	6.6	8.6	8.2
35-39 years	3.4	2.7	3.8	4.9	6.4	4.7
40-44 years	2.6	2.2	3.3	3.4	4.1	2.8

*No. moving out per 100 residing in South in 1955.

Source: U.S. Bureau of the Census. U.S. Census
of Population: 1960. Lifetime and Recent
Migration (Final Report PC(2)2D; Washington, D.C.: U.S. Government Printing
Office, 1963), Table 8.

Table 33

Per cent distribution of major occupation groups by education, color, and sex. persons twenty-five years of age and over, United States, 1960

| | White | | | | | | | Nonwhite | | | | | |
| | | White-collar | | | Blue- | | | | White-collar | | | Blue- | | |
	Total	Total	Prof., tech.	Other	collar	Agr.	NA	Total	Total	Prof., tech.	Other	collar	Agr.	NA
MEN														
Total	100	37	11	26	51	8	4	100	13	4	9	69	10	8
Under 11 years	100	19	2	17	66	10	5	100	6	1	5	73	13	8
12 years	100	41	7	34	49	6	4	100	21	3	18	66	3	10
13-15 years	100	67	20	47	26	4	3	100	40	13	27	49	2	9
16 years	100	86	42	44	9	2	3	100	72	47	25	20	1	7
17+ years	100	93	74	19	4	1	3	100	87	75	12	6	0	6
WOMEN														
Total	100	57	14	43	37	1	5	100	18	7	11	71	4	7
Under 11 years	100	33	2	31	59	2	6	100	5	1	4	82	5	8
12 years	100	71	7	64	24	1	4	100	30	6	24	61	1	8
13-15 years	100	84	31	53	10	1	5	100	55	20	35	38	--	7
16 years	100	92	69	23	3	--	5	100	87	74	13	8	--	5
17+ years	100	94	84	10	2	--	4	100	92	86	6	3	--	5

Source: U.S. Bureau of the Census. U.S. Census of Population: 1960. Educational Attainment (Final Report PC(2)5B; Washington, D.C.: U.S. Government Printing Office, 1963), Table 8.

179

Table 34

Percentage distribution of college graduates in teaching and other occupations, by color and sex, United States, 1960

	Males		Females	
	White	Nonwhite	White	Nonwhite
16 years of schooling				
Total	100	100	100	100
Professional and technical	42	47	69	74
Teachers, elementary and secondary schools	6	21	56	67
Other professional and technical	36	26	13	7
All other occupations	58	53	31	26
17+ years of schooling				
Total	100	100	100	100
Professional and technical	74	75	84	86
Teachers, elementary and secondary schools	13	21	50	60
Other professional and technical	61	54	34	26
All other occupations	26	25	16	14

Source: U.S. Bureau of the Census. U.S. Census of Population: 1960. Educational Attainment (Final Report PC(2)5B), Table 8; and Characteristics of Teachers (Final Report PC(2)7D), Table 4 (Washington, D.C.: U.S. Government Printing Office, 1963 and 1964).

APPENDIX B

METHODOLOGY

APPENDIX B METHODOLOGY

DETERMINING LONG-RUN TRENDS
IN EDUCATIONAL ATTAINMENT

The U.S. Censuses of Population in 1940, 1950, and 1960 reported--among other things--age, sex, and years of schooling. From these statistics we may discover past trends in schooling. For example, if a sixty-year-old man reported at the time of the 1960 Census that he had completed twelve years of school, or was a high school graduate, we know that he finished high school at about the time of World War I. Persons who reported having completed less than twelve years of schooling are not considered high school graduates; those who report thirteen or more years of schooling are judged to have entered college; and those who reported sixteen years or more are judged to have completed four years of college, and to be college graduates.

Hence, we can calculate for each age and sex group: the proportion who graduated from high school, the proportion of the high school graduates who entered college, and the proportion of

Table B.1

Proportions graduating from high school, college entrants, and college graduates, by sex and color: United States, about 1875 to 1955

MALES

Age group 1940 census	Age group 1960 census	Approximate year of high school graduation	White						Nonwhite					
			% of age group who were H.S. graduates		% of H.S. graduates who entered college		% of college entrants who graduated		% of age group who were H.S. graduates		% of H.S. graduates who entered college		% of college entrants who graduated	
			1940 census	1960 census	1940 census	1960 census	1940 census	1960 census	1940 census	1960 census	1940 census	1960 census	1940 census	1960 census
0- 4	20-24	1955	*	64.8	*	*	*	*	*	39.0	*	*	*	*
5- 9	25-29	1950	*	62.7	*	46.5	*	53.6	*	36.2	*	37.2	*	39.4
10-14	30-34	1945	*	56.2	*	48.0	*	58.5	*	29.8	*	39.7	*	46.3
15-19	35-39	1940	*	55.8	*	44.2	*	56.8	*	26.7	*	37.0	*	45.6
20-24	40-44	1935	*	49.9	*	41.2	*	52.0	*	21.4	*	37.0	*	45.1
25-29	45-49	1930	38.4	41.4	38.2	43.6	50.6	51.2	10.5	15.5	36.2	39.4	38.0	46.2
30-34	50-54	1925	33.3	34.7	45.3	49.2	53.6	51.5	8.6	12.4	42.8	42.5	44.4	44.2
35-39	55-59	1920	26.3	27.8	49.2	52.3	54.2	51.0	6.8	9.8	46.1	40.0	46.6	43.5
40-44	60-64	1915	23.2	23.8	48.8	53.0	51.3	47.8	6.5	8.7	48.1	47.2	46.2	44.1
45-49	65-69	1910	20.5	20.0	49.4	54.2	51.3	47.0	5.8	6.8	47.6	49.5	50.0	45.1a
50-54	70-74	1905	18.4	17.4	50.0	54.9	53.3	46.6	5.2	7.1	50.0	48.8	50.0a	46.5a
55-59	75+	1900	16.6	16.0	49.0	53.3	53.3	47.5	5.2	6.0	50.4	48.0	52.6a	46.4a
60-64		1895	15.8	*	50.4	*	53.8	*	4.9	*	51.3a	*	52.5a	*
65-69		1890	12.4	*	51.9	*	53.7	*	3.3	*	52.9a	*	b	*
70-74		1885	12.6	*	51.9	*	53.6	*	2.9	*	56.0a	*	b	*
75+		1880 and earlier	10.9	*	51.8	*	53.2	*	2.3	*	b	*	b	*

FEMALES

0- 4		*	*	*	*	*	*	*	44.7	*	*	*	*	*	
5- 9	1955	68.1	*	30.6	*	*	40.9	*	40.6	*	31.0	*	42.7	
10-14	1950	64.8	*	30.5	38.8	40.8	*	35.2	*	31.2	*	43.3	
15-19	1945	61.1	*	29.0	38.1	37.5	*	30.3	*	30.2	*	44.4	
20-24	1940	59.8	*	30.8	37.9	39.8	*	23.2	*	34.4	*	47.2	
20-24	1935	52.8	*											

Age	Year														
25-29	1930	45.1	43.4	31.3	35.9	38.9	41.2	13.7	17.7	34.8	38.0	36.6	49.1	
30-34	1925	39.5	38.0	38.5	42.8	38.8	40.3	11.0	14.8	42.3	42.6	36.0	49.3	
35-39	1920	32.7	31.6	40.6	45.3	38.1	38.3	8.6	11.5	41.3	42.8	36.9	46.5	
40-44	1915	27.8	27.4	40.1	45.0	38.1	36.9	7.3	10.3	41.9	43.2	38.5	42.1	
45-49	1910	23.7	23.5	40.7	46.0	37.9	34.3	6.8	8.1	41.6	45.2	40.0[a]	41.6	

50-54	1905	21.4	21.2	39.7	45.0	38.0	33.2	5.5	8.0	40.9	46.6	40.6[a]	39.5[a]	
55-59	1900	20.5	19.5	33.0	41.4	37.2	33.2	5.1	6.3	43.3[a]	44.4	35.7[a]	40.4[a]	
60-64	1895	*	15.7	38.2	*	37.3	*	4.4	*	42.9[a]	*	b	*	
65-69	1890	*	16.5	38.0	*	36.4	*	2.8	*	43.9[a]	*	b	*	
70-74	1885	*	15.0	36.7	*	36.7	*	2.2	*	b	*	b	*	
75+	1880 and earlier	*	13.3	38.0	*	37.7	*	1.3	*	b	*	b	*	

---

*Not applicable.

[a]Less than 10,000 cases in denominator.

[b]Too few cases for statistical reliability.

Sources: Sixteenth Census of the United States: 1940, Vol. IV, Characteristics by Age, Part I: United States Summary, Table 18; U.S. Census of Population: 1960. Detailed Characteristics. United States Summary (Final Report PC(1)1D), Table 174; and U.S. Census of Population: 1960. Educational Attainment (Final Report PC(2)5B), Table 2 (Washington, D.C.: U.S. Government Printing Office, 1963).

185

those who entered college who subsequently completed four years.

Statistics from both the 1960 and 1940 population censuses were used in order to cover a
longer time period. The population aged seventy-
five and over in 1940 was of high school graduation age approximately sixty years earlier, or
about 1875. The younger persons, those who graduated from high school after 1940, could be studied
only through the 1960 census data. In addition,
by comparing proportions for the two censuses, we
could gain some insight into the possible effects
of differences in reporting, as well as differences stemming from mortality. For example, 38
per cent of white males 25-29 years of age in 1940
reported completing high school. By 1960 this age
cohort was 45-49 years of age, and 41 per cent
then reported completing high school. The slight
differences do not affect the trends reported,
however, since the long-run changes as shown by
both censuses are very similar (Table B.1).

THE THREE QUESTIONNAIRE SURVEYS

We shall discuss in considerable detail the
three independent, but mutually supplementary,
mail questionnaire surveys which comprised the
greater portion of our research efforts. Since
the projections to 1975 of the educational attainment of Southern Negro youth have little in common methodologically with the three surveys, that
portion of the research is considered separately.

The material relevant to this section falls
under five main headings, as follows: I. Survey
of primarily Negro college students; II. Survey
of Southern Negro high school graduates intending
to enter college; III. Survey of Negro college
enrollments, student recruitment, student admissions, and student financing; IV. Common

problems for the three surveys, and how they were
met; and V. General evaluation of the surveys.

The fourth topic merits separate discussion,
since all three surveys did present common problems, quite apart from problems specific to each
survey, discussed under headings (I) through
(III). Chief among the common problems was that
of securing adequate questionnaire returns, and
(IV) is consequently primarily devoted to the
problem of "follow-up" for each of the surveys.
Two of the surveys attempted to obtain student
test-score data, and the section concludes with
a discussion of the problems encountered.

For each survey there are four principal
topics which we review in sequence: a) The relevant survey universe; b) Sampling from that universe; c) The returns for the sample; and d)
Adequacy of response for various questionnaire
items.

I. Survey of Students in
Primarily Negro Colleges

General Description of Survey

During the Summer of 1965 we sampled from a
universe of 104 primarily Negro colleges, the
great majority of which are located in the South,
and we subsequently secured questionnaires from
students enrolled in sixty-eight of these colleges. In each college we sampled from the total
student body enrolled, freshmen through seniors,
and finally received a total of 8,599 completed
questionnaires.

The student questionnaire was printed on two
sides of a single legal-sized sheet, and consisted
of twenty-three separate questions, most of them
precoded (see Exhibits at the end of this book).

The questions may be divided into three groups,
as follows: a) About the student--sex, race,
age, high school class standing, etc.; b) About
the student's family--education and occupation of
parents, and family income; and c) About the
student's college career and post-college plans--
financing of college, college major, expected
occupation, expected region of residence, and so
forth.

The essential aim of this survey of students
in primarily Negro colleges was to describe these
students with regard to their personal and background characteristics, and their future plans,
with special reference to the type and quality of
college they were attending.

We were able to classify the sixty-eight
colleges by type--public and private Southern
Negro four-year accredited colleges, Southern
Negro four-year nonaccredited colleges, Southern
Negro two-year colleges, and primarily Negro
colleges out of the South. We were able to
classify the four-year institutions as either
"good," "fair," or "poor" ones, using the quality
ratings developed by six experts on Negro colleges in the early 1960's. (See Appendix C for
a discussion of this quality rating.)

The Survey Universe

The original list of primarily Negro colleges
was furnished by the College Entrance Examination
Board. Since our study was concerned with undergraduates only, we excluded from the list two
medical schools, as well as the four exclusively
post-graduate schools of Atlanta University.
Several two-year colleges on the list were no
longer in existence, Summer, 1965. (See "Survey
Universe" in Section III of this appendix). We cannot claim that the final list of 104 undergraduate
colleges represents the exact total of such

colleges, but only a close approximation of the
total. In the course of our study we came to hear
of several additional colleges which one or
another of a variety of educational agencies or
authorities have included in their totals. In
fact, we have found no two lists of primarily
Negro colleges which completely agree. This is
the case since a proportion of these colleges
apparently have a rather tenuous existence, and
are included or excluded from lists according to
the particular standards set by the compiler of
the list.

Sampling from the Universe of Primarily Negro Colleges

Given the financial limits and the time
limits inherent in the design of our study, it
soon became apparent that we could not hope to
obtain questionnaire returns for all students enrolled in primarily Negro colleges. According to
the Office of Education, as reported in the
Statistical Abstract, there were approximately
100,000 such undergraduates enrolled in 1964.
Rather, we would have to sample so as to obtain
both a representative cross section of the universe of colleges and a representative group of
students from each college in the sample of colleges.

We first allocated each of the 104 colleges
in the universe to four groups according to type
of college: four-year public accredited, four-
year private accredited, four-year nonaccredited,
and two-year. We further subdivided each of the
four groups of colleges into two additional
groups: colleges in communities of under 100,000
persons, and colleges in communities of 100,000 or
more persons. Each of the resultant eight groups
of colleges was then divided into groups determined by size of enrollment, the number of enrollment groups for each of the eight type and

community-size groups being determined by the
range in college size within each group. We next
randomly selected sixty-six colleges from the
stratified universe, approximately proportional
to the total number appearing in each of the sub-
groups we have just defined. This number of colleges represented the total which we felt we could
reasonably handle within budgetary and time
limits, and which at the same time would yield a
reasonably representative cross section of the
types and sizes of primarily Negro colleges, and
of colleges within large and small communities.

We next wrote to these sixty-six colleges,
requesting their cooperation in administering our
questionnaire to samples of students enrolled in
Fall, 1965-1966. (See Exhibits.) After several
weeks we followed up the original letter by an
additional one, and then by phone calls to the
colleges from which we had received no replies.

Fifty-three of the sixty-six colleges finally
agreed to participate in the study and in fact did
so, returning completed student questionnaires to
us. We felt, however, that additional colleges
were needed to form a balanced sample, and selec-
tively approached colleges of the types and sizes
which were deficient. Fifteen additional colleges
agreed to participate and later returned completed
questionnaires.

The final sample from the universe of colleges, then, consisted of sixty-eight primarily
Negro colleges. Table B.2 indicates the distributions of the universe of colleges and the colleges
which participated in our study, according to type
and size of college, and size of the community in
which the college is located. The various types
and sizes of colleges are all well represented,
as are the community sizes, with the exception of
large nonaccredited colleges in small communities,
and possibly small two-year colleges in large

Table B.2

Numbers of colleges by type, enrollment size, and size of community

Type of college

| Enrollment and size of community | 4-year accredited | | | | 4-year nonaccredited | | 2-year | |
| | Public | | Private | | | | | |
	College universe	Colleges partici-pating	College universe	Colleges partici-pating	College universe	Colleges partici-pating	College universe	Colleges partici-pating
Under 1,000 students								
Community under 100,000	9	6	18	14	9	6	18	11
Community 100,000 or more	--	--	13	9	2	2	5	2
1,000 or more students								
Community under 100,000	14	6	2	2	2	--	--	--
Community 100,000 or more	7	6	4	3	1	1	--	--

communities. A list of the specific colleges in
the sample (names as at the time of our survey),
and their location by state, follows.

Alabama

      Alabama State College
      Miles College
      Oakwood College
      Stillman College
      Talladega College
      Tuskegee Institute

Arkansas

      Agricultural, Mechanical and Normal College
      Philander Smith College

Delaware

      Delaware State College

District of Columbia

      Howard University

Florida

      Edward Waters College
      Florida Normal and Industrial Memorial
        College
      Hampton Junior College
      Jackson Junior College
      Johnson Junior College
      Rosenwald Junior College
      Suwanee River Junior College
      Volusia County Community College

Georgia

   Albany State College
   Clark College
   Morehouse College
   Morris Brown College
   Paine College
   Savannah State College

Kentucky

   Kentucky State College

Louisiana

   Grambling College
   Xavier University

Maryland

   Coppin State College
   Maryland State College
   Morgan State College

Mississippi

   Alcorn Agricultural and Mechanical College
   Coahoma Junior College
   Jackson State College
   Mississippi Industrial College
   Natchez Junior College
   Piney Woods Country Life School
   Prentiss Normal and Industrial Institute
   Rust College
   T. J. Harris Junior College
   Tougaloo College

(cont.)

North Carolina

Agricultural and Technical College of North
    Carolina
Elizabeth City State College
Fayetteville State Teachers College
Johnson C. Smith University
Livingstone College
Saint Augustine's College
Shaw University
Winston-Salem State College

Ohio

Wilberforce University

Oklahoma

Langston University

Pennsylvania

Lincoln University

South Carolina

Claflin College
Voorhees College

Tennessee

Fisk University
Knoxville College
Lane College
Owen College
Tennessee Agricultural and Industrial State
    University

Texas

Bishop College
Huston-Tillotson College
Jarvis Christian College
Paul Quinn College
St. Philip's College
Texas College
Wiley College

Virginia

    Hampton Institute
    Virginia State College
    Virginia Union University

Sampling from the Students Enrolled in the Sixty-Eight Colleges

Our initial problem in terms of sampling the students enrolled in the sixty-eight colleges was to obtain a sufficient number of students attending each type of college for a reliable statistical analysis. Since some type-groups included generally larger colleges than did others, we therefore totalled the college enrollments for each type-group and determined upon specific proportions of these totals as our respondent goals. We hoped to obtain returns from 20 per cent of the students in the four-year private accredited colleges, 10 per cent of those in the four-year public accredited colleges, 30 per cent of the students in the four-year nonaccredited colleges, and one third of the students enrolled in the two-year colleges.

It was then possible to determine the number of student-respondents needed for each individual college. For example, we wished to obtain responses from 20 per cent of the students in each of the four-year private accredited colleges. The number of student-respondents was then varied according to the size of the college, assuring that each college within a college type-group would be represented to the extent that it contributed to the total of students in the type-group.

From directories we had already determined the proportions of Negroes whose last names commenced with the various letters of the alphabet. Therefore, for each college we were able to determine how many students should have last names

commencing with the various letters. For each
college, starting with a randomly selected letter
of the alphabet, we simply summed the number of
students for this and each successive letter until
we reached the desired number for a particular
college. In point of fact, we systematically
oversampled for each college, anticipating that
some students, for a variety of reasons, would be
lost to the study during the process of administering the questionnaire. This precaution proved
to be wise, since the final number of returns fell
considerably short of what the original calcula-
tions led us to expect as the maximum possible
number of returns.

We do not pretend that the sampling procedure
assured us a perfect sample by any means, but only
that it guarded against major biases. The limits
on sampling were at once a lack of precise data on
the universe of colleges, and the necessity of de-
vising a means of selecting students that college
officials could easily follow in administering the
questionnaire, since we were dependent on them for
following our instructions. By and large we feel
that they did so, but we are also certain that the
sample would have been somewhat improved had we
been able to afford to send our own personnel to
each college to administer the data collection
procedures.

To a considerable extent, we were able to
judge whether each particular college had followed
instructions or not, using information on the
questionnaires returned as the criteria. For
example, one large college returned to us a sample
consisting entirely of freshmen. Subsequent communications with this college revealed that our
instructions had been misunderstood, and the college obligingly distributed questionnaires to a
proper sample of students. This error was the
most serious one that came to our attention.

For the three most important types of colleges the numbers of students ranged from just under 1,100 in four-year Southern nonaccredited colleges to just under 3,200 for four-year private accredited Southern colleges. There are a little over 3,100 respondents for four-year public colleges. According to the Office of Education, well over 90 per cent of the students enrolled in primarily Negro colleges in 1964 were attending these three categories of schools. Just under 90 per cent of our respondents were attending such schools, and for all three types there are sufficient numbers for extensive analysis.

Limitations of the Data

First, there is reason to believe that we have an undue proportion of freshman respondents, but it is difficult to judge the extent of this bias. For colleges which are expanding rapidly it is difficult to determine (without visiting the college) how large the freshman class should be, compared to upper classes.

Second, we appear to have received questionnaires from an undue proportion of women, and here we are better able to estimate the extent of the error. About 12 out of 20 of the respondents are women, whereas the Office of Education reported about 11 women in every 20 students enrolled in primarily Negro colleges, 1964.

Perhaps women are more responsive to requests to fill out questionnaires. Perhaps the entering freshmen are more easily located than upperclassmen, and hence were unduly represented.

Data were obtained for only two primarily Negro colleges out of the South. Though the universe of such colleges is a small one, we cannot claim that these two schools describe it precisely. However, the characteristics of the

students attending these two schools were so very
different from those of students attending colleges within the South that we finally tabulated
them separately. The 229 students responding from
the two colleges form a small and numerically un-
important group; however, this sub-sample is
interesting in that the students in these Northern
Negro colleges very probably differ from those in
Southern ones in many respects.

We cannot say that our total sample of students exactly represents the total universe of
students in primarily Negro colleges. Comparing
our returns with Office of Education figures for
a year earlier, we appear to have oversampled two-
year college students and students in four-year
private colleges, and undersampled students in
four-year public colleges. As already pointed
out, our sampling procedure primarily attempted
to obtain sufficient students in each category of
college for statistical analysis, regardless of
the proportion of the total universe each category
represents. Accordingly, we do not present tabulations for the total sample, but rather for the
sub-samples independently. Percentaging is for
the total in each category, and oversampling or
undersampling therefore does not affect findings
for sub-samples, or comparisons between sub-
samples.

In Section III of this appendix we describe
in detail the recent and extensive merging of two-
year public Negro colleges, especially in Florida,
with neighboring primarily white two-year colleges. Several of these colleges had already
merged at the time we asked colleges to administer
the student questionnaire. A number had not yet
merged, and for these schools, still enrolling
students in the Fall of 1965, questionnaires were
obtained. To the extent that this is true, the
findings for two-year colleges in this survey are
essentially of historical interest. We can only

observe that in consequence to the mergers, the characteristics reported for students in two-year primarily Negro colleges would increasingly apply to Negro students in two-year Southern integrated colleges.

Negro Students in Southern Integrated Colleges

Initially, we attempted to obtain question-naire data for Negro students attending integrated colleges in the South. For a number of reasons, this attempt was not very successful. Data were finally obtained from ninety students in three colleges, and tabulations for this sub-sample are presented separately. We do not claim, of course, that this small number of students at a few colleges represents the universe of Negro students at Southern integrated colleges. We present the statistics, therefore, with a minimum of comment, and leave their interpretation largely to the reader. We will briefly describe, however, the difficulties encountered in attempting to gain data on students in integrated schools.

In the first place, there is a paucity of reliable information on numbers of Negroes enrolled in Southern primarily white colleges. It is therefore difficult to establish the relevant universe of colleges, or to determine how to sample from the colleges.

Furthermore, we were advised that the colleges themselves would not favor interviewing Negro students for a variety of reasons, and we therefore attempted to approach persons within the college communities who would locate the students and interview them. This proved extremely difficult and, after following up a number of leads, we eventually obtained only this inadequate sample.

In general, it can only be said that an adequate study of Negro students enrolled at primarily white Southern colleges would require far more money than we had, and would just as certainly require sending study personnel to the colleges to supervise, or even personally administer, the field work.

In sum, the only reliable data we have on Negro students attending integrated colleges derives from our survey of Southern Negro high school graduates entering college in Fall, 1965, described in the second section of this appendix.

Completeness and Quality of the Questionnaire Responses

For most of the questionnaire items very high proportions of usable answers were obtained, but for a few items there were large proportions of "nonascertainables" or "don't know's." For these problem questions we indicate below the proportion of respondents failing to supply data:

Questionnaire item	Per cent failing to supply data
Student's rank in high school class	23
Father's occupation	26
Father's education	9
Family income	33

We cannot say, for these questions, whether students failing to supply data differ systematically from those supplying data; therefore the

reader is urged to interpret with caution differences of a few percentage points on tables including these variables. Students from lower
socio-economic backgrounds were the most likely
to omit items of information.

Apart from the "problem items" just mentioned, we have every reason to believe that the
data are quite reliable. Most of the questions,
such as sex, age, and year in college, were ones
of simple fact. Responses concerning occupational plans and expected region of residence
undoubtedly express the students' opinions and
feelings.

II. Survey of Southern Negro High
School Graduates Planning on
College Entrance in Fall, 1965
(Excluding Graduates from the Border States)

General Description of Survey

During the Summer of 1965 questionnaires were
sent to each of 1,831 Southern Negro high schools,
excepting those in the border states, requesting
information regarding their Spring, 1965, graduates intending to enter college the following
Fall. (See Exhibits.) We also asked for the size
of the graduating class. These high school data
supplemented information from our college questionnaire for students enrolled in primarily Negro
colleges, Fall, 1965. We could tabulate, for example, the proportions of the high school graduates entering integrated (primarily white) colleges out of the South--information the college
questionnaire could not provide. It was also
feasible to relate the characteristics of the high
schools--size, location, and proportion of graduates entering college--to the type, quality, and
location of the college. Finally, we could relate
some characteristics of the high school graduates--

sex, rank in class, and aptitude or achievement test standing according to national norms--to these same college variables.

The Survey Universe

The survey universe consists of all Negro high schools in states where less than 8 per cent of Negroes were attending schools with whites, 1964-1965. The relevant states are all Southern, excepting the border states of Maryland, Delaware, West Virginia, Kentucky, Missouri, Oklahoma, and the District of Columbia, all of which are omitted. The least integrated of the states excluded had just over 30 per cent of Negro children enrolled in schools with whites, and the most integrated had fully 88 per cent.

Five of the relevant states--Arkansas, Alabama, Mississippi, Georgia, and South Carolina--had less than 1 per cent of Negroes enrolled in schools with whites. These are the states which we call the "deep South" in this study. They are all geographically contiguous. The remaining relevant states with 1 to 7 per cent of Negroes enrolled in schools with whites--what we term "other South"--geographically surround the "deep South," and include Florida, Louisiana, Texas, Tennessee, North Carolina, and Virginia.

The universe represents, then, the great majority, but not all, of Negro high schools. Conversely, for the relevant states, graduates of Negro high schools represent the overwhelming majority of Negro children graduating from high school.

We located the specific high schools falling into the universe by means of state lists of such schools furnished us by the College Entrance Examination Board. The Negro high schools on the lists were distributed as follows:

Initial Survey Universe of Negro High Schools

Location of high school	Number	Per cent
"Deep South"	798	43.6
"Other South"	1,033	56.4
Both locations	1,831	100.0

We should point out that the 1,831 high schools to which we mailed questionnaires, representing all schools on the list furnished us, do not precisely represent the probable universe of Negro high schools, if for no other reason than that there may be some Negro high schools not on our initial list and, therefore, irrevocably lost to us. We subsequently discovered that some schools on the list had closed down, others had become exclusively elementary schools or schools for exceptional children. A few turned out to be white schools. The 1,831 high schools compose the initial or "mailing" universe.

Sampling from the Initial Universe
of Negro High Schools

We first sent questionnaires, plus an explanatory letter, to every fourth school on the state lists. Returns were too few from this mailing, however, and we subsequently sent an identical mailing to the balance of the high schools on the lists. From the two mailings we received 203 responses from high schools, or 11 per cent of the total of 1,831 schools.

The 203 schools responding reported on just over 3,600 students planning to enter college in

Fall, 1965, or about eighteen students per high
school. The number of students was clearly adequate for the tabulations we planned, but the
representativeness of an 11 per cent sample of the
high schools was just as clearly open to question.
Given the initial low rate of response, it was
beyond our financial means and time limitations
to secure returns from the two thirds or better of
all the schools necessary to assure a reasonably
representative sample.

Instead, we attempted to obtain a 100 per
cent response from a sample of fifty of the
schools on the list. The characteristics of the
schools, and the students enrolled, in the sample
of fifty would provide an index of the representativeness of the larger sample when compared to
those of the larger group of returns. Accordingly
fifty high schools were selected from the lists--
every thirty-seventh school--and each was sent a
questionnaire and an explanatory letter. Four high
schools fell both in the large sample and the
sample of fifty, and were retained in both places,
since the samples were independently drawn.

After extensive follow-up mailings, plus
numerous phone calls, we managed to account for
all fifty high schools. For forty of them we
obtained usable questionnaire returns. Five
turned out to be predominantly white high schools.
The remaining five failed to return questionnaires
for various reasons, such as having closed down,
having ceased to enroll high school level students, and so forth.

We can now compare responses for the forty
returns from the sample of fifty and the larger
sample. Nonexistent schools, and schools that had
ceased to be high schools, of course were not included in the larger sample--and internal questionnaire evidence had permitted us to locate and,
after telephone verification, eliminate white high
schools from the larger sample. It remained to

adjust our initial or "mailing" universe to accord with the sample of fifty, the sample of schools for which we had 100 per cent information.

In the following section we present the "mailing" universe adjusted to accord with the sample of fifty--and we then compare the sample of fifty with the larger sample to estimate the representativeness of the latter.

Estimated Probable Universe

In the first table on the following page the original "mailing" universe was adjusted according to findings for the sample of fifty schools for which complete information was obtained.

In the second table on the following page we can now make a three-way comparison by region between the number of Negro high schools in the estimated probable universe, the number in the sample of fifty, and the number in the larger sample.

So far as numbers of schools in the two sub-regions of the South are concerned, the two samples closely resemble each other, and both samples closely resemble the estimated probable universe of Negro high schools in these sub-regions.

The remaining question is whether the larger sample resembles the sample of fifty in terms of additional characteristics of the schools, as well as characteristics of the students--characteristics for which we have no direct information for the estimated probable universe.

Further Comparisons Between the Sample
of Fifty and the Larger Sample

First, how do the two samples compare with each other, for the two sub-regions of the South,

"Mailing Universe," Characteristics of Sample of Fifty High Schools, and Consequent Adjustment to Produce Estimated Probable Universe

Location of high school	"Mailing universe"	Sample of 50				Per cent to be removed from "mailing universe"	Estimated probable universe
		Valid returns	White schools	Closed, not a high school, etc.	Total		
	No.	No.	No.	No.	No.	%	No.
"Deep South"	798	17	3	1	21	19.04	646
"Other South"	1,033	23	2	4	29	20.69	819
Total	1,831	40	5	5	50		1,465

Number of High Schools

	Estimated probable universe		Sample of 50		Larger sample	
	No.	%	No.	%	No.	%
"Deep South"	646	44.1	17	42.5	89	43.8
"Other South"	819	55.9	23	57.5	114	56.2
Total	1,465	100.0	40	100.0	203	100.0

in terms of number of high school graduates
planning to enter college?

Number and Per Cent of High School Graduates
Planning to Enter College,
by Sub-Region of the South

	Sample of 50		Larger sample	
	No.	%	No.	%
"Deep South"	313	46.2	1,569	43.5
"Other South"	365	53.8	2,035	56.5
Total	678	100.0	3,604	100.0

The distribution of students planning to
enter college for the two subdivisions of the
South is very similar for both samples. Since
this was also the case for the number of schools
reporting, we believe that the large sample, in
spite of the low (11 per cent) rate of response,
was not unduly biased towards any one sub-region
of the South--nor were the schools responding
those which sent particularly large or small
groups of students on to college.

How do the two samples compare with regard to
sex of college entrants?

Number and Per Cent of High School Graduates
Entering College, by Sex of Graduate

	Sample of 50		Larger sample	
	No.	%	No.	%
Men	295	43.6	1,475	40.9
Women	381	56.4	2,128	59.1
Total	676	100.0	3,603	100.0

Once again the two distributions accord closely. The probability that the differences between the two samples are due to factors other than chance alone, according to the chi-square test of significance, is very small (p = .2).

The two samples were compared for seven additional variables, two of them measures of the student's academic status, and five of them characteristics of the colleges students expected to enter. The tabulations follow. For the two student variables and for four of the five college characteristics there are no significant differences between the two samples. For the fifth college variable, quality of college, there is a .01 chi-square probability that the differences between the two samples are not due to chance alone.

High School Class Standing of Student

	Sample of 50		Larger sample	
	No.	%	No.	%
Top half of class	482	74.5	2,694	75.9
Bottom half of class	165	25.5	853	24.1
Total	647	100.0	3,547	100.0
N.A.	31		57	

Test-Score Standing of Students
According to National Norms

	Sample of 50		Larger sample	
	No.	%	No.	%
Top half of national distribution	102	23.7	631	24.4
Bottom half of national distribution	329	76.3	1,957	75.6
Total	431	100.0	2,588	100.0
N.A.	247		1,016	

Control of College Student Is Entering

	Sample of 50		Larger sample	
	No.	%	No.	%
Public college	405	61.6	2,240	64.0
Private college	253	38.4	1,262	36.0
Total	658	100.0	3,502	100.0
N.A.	20		102	

Level of Offering of College Student Is Entering

	Sample of 50		Larger sample	
	No.	%	No.	%
Two-year college	116	17.2	594	16.7
Four-year college	559	82.8	2,963	83.3
Total	675	100.0	3,557	100.0
N.A.	3		47	

(cont.)

Color Status of College Student Is Entering

	Sample of 50		Larger sample	
	No.	%	No.	%
Primarily Negro	556	83.4	2,903	82.1
Primarily white	111	16.6	635	17.9
Total	667	100.0	3,538	100.0

Location of College Student Is Entering

	Sample of 50		Larger sample	
	No.	%	No.	%
"Deep South"	267	39.6	1,340	37.3
"Other South"	376	55.7	1,921	53.5
Border	20	3.0	200	5.6
Out of South	12	1.7	131	3.6
Total	675	100.0	3,592	100.0
N.A.	3		12	

Quality of College Student Is Entering
(Excludes integrated colleges and
two-year primarily Negro colleges)

	Sample of 50		Larger sample	
	No.	%	No.	%
"Good" four-year colleges	206*	42.0*	866	33.6
"Fair" four-year colleges	196	40.0	1,168	45.3
"Poor" four-year colleges	88	18.0	545	21.1
Total	490	100.0	2,579	100.0

*(65 students from a single high school all planned
on entering the State College, a "good" college)

210

In the last instance, we believe that the
sample of fifty is the misleading one. Only 490
students from this sample were entering four-year
Negro colleges, and of this total sixty-five students from a large high school, two thirds of the
graduates from this school entering college, were
all entering the local State College or its
branch, rated a "good" college. Apparently
graduates from this high school systematically
enter this one college, and given the small total
of cases in the sample of fifty schools, these
entrants unduly inflate the proportions entering
"good" colleges.

With the exception of the instance just discussed, the samples are in close accord for all of
the significant dependent and independent variables in the analysis. Accordingly, we simply
combined the two samples when we made tabulations,
since this afforded us the advantage of additional
numbers of cases.

Completeness and Quality of the Questionnaire Responses

In the tables comparing the two samples just
discussed, we include, at the bottom of each
table, the number of "nonascertainables" for that
particular variable. The missing data are given
on the following page.

In addition, our data on the high schools
themselves were virtually complete. In all instances we knew the location, and in almost all,
the size of the graduating class and the number of
entrants going on to college. In almost all instances we could derive the proportions going on
to college, and in all cases the size of the community in which the high school was located.

Variable	Number of "non-ascertainables" in the two samples combined	Per cent nonascertainable
High school class standing	88	2.1
Test-score standing of student	1,263	29.5
Sex of student	3	*
Control of college entered	122	2.8
Level of offering of college entered	50	1.2
Color status of college entered	77	1.8
Location of college entered	15	*
Quality of four-year** college entered	36	1.1
Total cases in combined samples	4,282	--

*Less than 1 per cent.

**There were 3,123 students enrolling in four-year colleges. No quality ratings were given to junior colleges.

The single instance of a large proportion of "nonascertainables" was that of student test-score data, where we had information for only about 7 out of 10 students because some schools apparently do not test their students, others do not keep

systematic records of all the students tested, and
others administer little known tests which cannot
be related to the standard tests in order to
arrive at national norms. There is no way of
knowing whether the 30 per cent of students for
whom we have no test data differ systematically
from those for whom data were obtained. We
strongly suspect that the students at less adequate high schools tended to be the ones who were
not tested, or for whom records were not kept if
they were tested. If this is the case, such students would probably have done relatively poorly
on tests; accordingly, if test data had been
available for them our main conclusions, drawn
from the available test data, would simply have
been strengthened.

The test-score data are the most troublesome.
We cannot say that this information is precise
enough for any refined analysis, and we do not
accept differences of a few percentage points as
significant when this variable is included in
cross-tabulations. An expert from the College
Entrance Examination Board related to each other
the various kinds of tests administered to the
students in different schools, using all available
specifications regarding the particular tests.
Students were accordingly placed in national quartile groups according to their scores.

Regarding the quality of the other items, we
can say that most of the information on the students, the high schools they attended, and the
colleges they proposed to enter was subject only
to the inevitable small percentage of clerical
error. This is certainly true of sex of student,
the college a particular student intended to
enter, the size of the community in which the high
school was located, and so forth. It is true even
of the student's rank in high school class, since
rank in class apparently is information almost all
high schools systematically record.

In general the two measures of academic status—test score and class rank—confirm each other. Almost all students in the top half of the national test-score distribution also ranked in the top half of their high school classes. Considered together, the two academic measures give a reasonable intellectual profile of the Southern Negro high school graduate who intends to enter college.

III. Survey of Negro College Enrollments,
      Student Recruitment and Admissions,
            and Student Financing

General Description of Survey

During the Winter of 1965-1966 we sent to 113* primarily Negro colleges in the South and in the states of Ohio and Pennsylvania a six-page questionnaire to be filled out by an official at each college (see Exhibits). The questions included: total enrollment, 1962 and 1965, and estimated 1968; applicants, acceptances, and new entrants, 1962 and 1965; college and government derived financial assistance to students; past, present, and contemplated recruitment of students; and admissions practices and preferences. The questionnaire was addressed to the president of the college in all instances, but the accompanying explanatory letter asked him to pass the questionnaire on to the person most familiar with the questionnaire items.

---

*To the 104 colleges on our original list we added nine more which were brought to our attention subsequently. Of the original universe of 116 colleges we already knew that three had merged with primarily white schools, and therefore did not send them questionnaires. All three of these colleges had been two-year public ones.

The Survey Universe

        In this survey, ninety-five colleges which
were sent questionnaires represent the total universe of primarily Negro colleges which we consider relevant to the purposes of the study. We
removed exclusively graduate institutions and professional schools since our study was concerned
with undergraduate students only. We finally excluded two-year public colleges also from the
survey for the following reasons:

        Although originally questionnaires were
mailed to the public two-year colleges, we soon
learned from the responses that these colleges
were rapidly merging with nearby formerly white
public two-year colleges. Almost all of these
mergers took place during the survey period, 1965-
1966. The following tabulation indicates the universe of public two-year colleges by location and
by whether or not they have merged with white
schools (as of July, 1966, to the best of our
knowledge):

Location of college	Universe of two-year public Negro colleges		
	Merged	Not merged	Total
Florida	9	3	12
Texas	1	–	1
South Carolina	1	–	1
Mississippi	–	1	1
Total	11	4	15

One additional two-year public college in North Carolina has not merged with a white school, but now has a predominantly white student body. In addition, since mergers in Florida seem to derive from statewide educational policy, we are doubtful how long the remaining three schools retaining separate identities will continue to remain separate. In brief, we saw little point in asking for information on future plans from the four remaining public two-year schools, and therefore excluded this category entirely from our analysis.

Two additional schools, both of them private junior colleges, were lost since they recently closed down; both schools were located in Mississippi.

The following table summarizes the original total list of colleges, and indicates the number lost for various reasons, and those remaining as the final universe for the "recruitment" questionnaire:

		Number of colleges
Original universe		116
Colleges lost to universe		
Medical schools	2	
Exclusively graduate schools	1	
Public two-year colleges	16	
Private two-year colleges	2	
Total lost to universe		21
Final universe		95

Returns from the Survey Universe

We received usable questionnaire returns from eighty-four of the ninety-five colleges in the final universe, or about 88 per cent of the total. The table on page 221 summarizes these returns, as well as the final universe, by numbers of colleges of various types and qualities. For each of the categories we include the number of students enrolled in 1965, as indicated by the college officials furnishing questionnaire enrollment data, and an estimate of the total enrollment. This estimate includes those colleges which failed to respond, but for whom enrollment figures were reported by the Office of Education in its annual directories of higher education. In short, our analysis is based on returns for 88 per cent of the colleges in the universe and on about 87 per cent of all the students enrolled.

The most deficient category in regard to proportion of the estimated total enrollment is the private two-year college. We omitted this group and limited our analysis to the four-year schools.

A complete list of the four-year colleges from which usable returns were obtained follows:

Alabama

        Alabama Agricultural & Mechanical College
        Alabama State College
        Miles College
        Oakwood College
        Stillman College
        Talladega College
        Tuskegee Institute

                                    (cont.)

Arkansas

    Agricultural, Mechanical and Normal College
    Arkansas Baptist College
    Philander Smith College
    Shorter College

Delaware

    Delaware State College

District of Columbia

    Howard University

Florida

    Bethune-Cookman College
    Edward Waters College
    Florida Agricultural & Mechanical University
    Florida Normal & Industrial Memorial College

Georgia

    Albany State College
    Clark College
    Fort Valley State College
    Morehouse College
    Morris Brown College
    Paine College
    Savannah State College
    Spelman College

Kentucky

    Kentucky State College

Louisiana

    Dillard University
    Southern University in Baton Rouge
    Southern University in New Orleans
    Xavier University

Maryland

    Bowie State College
    Coppin State College
    Maryland State College
    Morgan State College

Mississippi

    Alcorn Agricultural & Mechanical College
    Jackson State College
    Mississippi Industrial College
    Mississippi Valley State College
    Rust College
    Tougaloo College

North Carolina

    Agricultural & Technical College of North
        Carolina
    Barber-Scotia College
    Bennett College
    Fayetteville State College
    Johnson C. Smith University
    Livingstone College
    Saint Augustine's College
    Shaw University
    Winston-Salem State College

Ohio

    Wilberforce University

Oklahoma

    Langston University

Pennsylvania

    Cheyney State College
    Lincoln University

(cont.)

South Carolina

  Allen University
  Morris College
  South Carolina State College
  Voorhees College

Tennessee

  Knoxville College
  Lane College
  Le Moyne College
  Tennessee Agricultural and Industrial State
      University

Texas

  Bishop College
  Butler College
  Huston-Tillotson College
  Jarvis Christian College
  Paul Quinn College
  Prairie View Agricultural & Mechanical
      College
  Texas College
  Wiley College

Virginia

  Hampton Institute
  Virginia State College
  Virginia Union University

West Virginia

  Bluefield State College
  West Virginia State College

Summary of Survey Returns

	Final universe - No. of colleges	Estimated enrollment	Questionnaire returns - No. of colleges	Reported enrollment	% of estimated enrollment
4-year public accredited colleges	31	63,486	27	53,361	84
4-year private accredited colleges	36	35,022	32	31,700	91
4-year nonaccredited colleges	15	10,187	15	10,187	100
2-year private colleges	13	2,847	10	2,012	71
All types of 4-year colleges	95	111,542	84	97,260	87
"Good"	20	31,064	18	27,260	88
"Fair"	31	51,291	27	43,428	85
"Poor"	31	26,340	29	24,560	93

Completeness and Quality of
the Questionnaire Responses

In general, the college officials who filled
out the questionnaires did so with a great deal of
care and with very few omissions. For example, we
have 1962 and 1965 enrollment figures for all
eighty-four colleges, and estimated 1968 enrollment figures for all except two colleges. We have
both 1962 and 1965 new entrant data for all except
four colleges (1968 estimates were not requested
for new entrants).

There is good reason to believe that the
figures are generally reliable as well as relatively complete. The figures, in most cases
neatly typed in, are exact ones rather than
approximations (e.g., "1,461" rather than "1,500").
From communications with college officials in the
course of the study it became clear that the
figures asked for are ones that are carefully kept
by the colleges for their own use, as well as for
the outside agencies that request these data. To
the extent that we can compare them, our totals
accord with those of other agencies reporting
similar statistics, such as the Office of Education.

The student loan and work-study program data
appear similarly reliable and complete. Since the
colleges themselves enter these programs, records
of participating students are a part of normal
record keeping. This, of course, is equally true
of scholarships deriving from the colleges themselves.

The sections of the questionnaire devoted to
recruitment of students and admissions practices
and preferences also had almost no omissions of
requested information, and the questions themselves were apparently understood in the senses in
which intended. If there are any significant deficiencies in this regard, they relate to groups

or types of students *especially* preferred. Many
of the officials checked a large number of groups,
and occasional comments such as: "We of course
want all groups"--lead us to believe that there
was some reluctance regarding specific commitments
on this question.

By and large, however, we feel that the information we received is both reliable in terms of
the statistics entered, and representative of the
actual practices, plans, and preferences of the
colleges. In large measure we feel that this is
so because the questionnaires were filled out by
high ranking officials at the colleges--in many
cases by the presidents themselves.

IV.   The Major Problems for
the Three Surveys

The Reluctant Respondents

The greatest problem encountered in the
entire study was that of "follow-up." For all
three surveys initial mailings requesting partici-
pation in the study, or requesting data, failed to
secure a sufficient response. Second mailings
also left deficiencies, and we then were forced to
contact high schools or colleges, as the case
might be, by telephone. The problem was far less
one of refusals than that the schools and colleges
simply failed to contact us. For example, only
ten Negro colleges directly refused to assist in
obtaining data on the students enrolled. For the
survey of college entrants from Negro high schools,
all fifty of the colleges in the validation sample
of fifty (the only one we followed up) ultimately
were accounted for. In the survey of Negro college enrollments and recruitment no single college
told us that it refused to fill in the brief
questionnaire; eleven simply failed to return
questionnaires after they had repeatedly assured
us we could expect returns in the near future.

In this section we would first like to explain why the data were so difficult to obtain, as
we see it from cumulative evidence over the survey
period, and then describe the extent of the
follow-up effort that proved necessary for each of
the surveys.

Obtaining data through mail surveys is, of
course, more difficult than when respondents are
approached in person. But the expense of con-
ducting field work is extremely high, especially
when, as was the case for our study, there were
very large numbers of high schools and colleges
in many different and widely separated locations.

But it was not simply the fact that it is
easy to forget or mislay mail requests for data
that created our data-gathering problems. First,
for the Negro colleges, rapid expansion has apparently meant a very great increase in administra-
tive and clerical work. With the best of inten-
tions, many colleges found it difficult to devote
time and attention to our requests for information.
In addition, obtaining the student data was admittedly a considerable undertaking for the college staff. We encountered least difficulty in
obtaining returns for the "recruitment" questionnaire, a single brief document which could be
filled out to a great extent from records con-
veniently on file as part of standard procedures.

Secondly, in the course of the study it was
learned that requests to the Negro colleges for
data have been increasing very rapidly over the
last several years. Apparently current concern
over higher education for Negroes has led to a
mounting number of separate studies of the colleges and their students, each of which represents
increased demands on the time of the college personnel. While understanding the reasons for this
development, time and again college officials com-
plained of the additional burden. In a number of

instances our study was confused with ones being
conducted by other research agencies.

For the high schools, the chief difficulty,
apart from simply forgetting or setting aside the
mailing, was difficulty in assembling the student
data from incomplete, scattered, or in some cases
nonexistent records.

There was a brief initial period of phone
contact with colleges in Summer, 1965, in which
we spoke with officials in Negro colleges in our
initial sample who had failed to respond to two
mail requests for cooperation.

Follow-up on participating colleges which had
failed to return student questionnaires commenced
in mid-Fall, 1965, and continued through Winter,
1965-1966. The high schools were first sent
questionnaires in October, 1965. A second mailing
followed some weeks later, and finally the small
validation sample of fifty schools was approached.
Follow-up on this small sample continued until
mid-Spring, 1966. Follow-up on the "recruitment"
questionnaire continued longest, terminating at
about the time many colleges closed for the Summer,
in early June, 1966.

It was necessary to phone over forty high
schools in the sample of fifty, and about sixty
colleges to whom recruitment questionnaires were
sent. Combining the phone calls necessary to enlist the cooperation of colleges administering
the college student questionnaire, those necessary
to track down failures to return questionnaires,
and those necessary to follow up requests for
student test-score data (a separate mailing), we
contacted over fifty colleges by phone for this
survey (characteristics of students enrolled in
college).

In addition, there were a considerable number
of phone calls necessary to check ambiguous data

on one or another of the survey returns. Ostensible Negro high schools which appeared to be primarily white schools from the questionnaire data were phoned to confirm this surmise.

At first glance it would seem that many colleges could be phoned regarding both the "recruitment" and the student questionnaires at the same time. This, however, proved largely impractical, since the same officials were seldom responsible for the two surveys.

The mere task of locating the college or school officials responsible often required several phone calls, and if the proper official was not available at the time of a call, a further call, or calls, became necessary.

Our estimate is that about 150 educational institutions were called on the phone in order to secure adequate returns for the three surveys, and that each institution was called, on the average, about three separate times.

Since calls had to be made in the daytime, day rates prevailed, and we estimate that each call cost about an average of $2.50.

In brief, follow-up was extremely expensive in terms of phone bills. In addition, phone follow-up required a person to make the calls. Since less than four calls could be placed per hour, the salary expenditure was also considerable. We do not know whether having personnel in the field would have proven less expensive, but we do believe that this possibility should be borne in mind by researchers in this area in the future. Aside from expense, the protracted follow-up period meant delays in coding and tabulating returns, and ultimately in making the analysis.

The Problem of Obtaining Test-Score Data for the Primarily Negro College Students

We originally intended to obtain test-score data for both the sample of students attending primarily Negro colleges and the Negro high school graduates entering college. The student scores for the various tests, adjusted to conform to national norms, would tell us how the various groups of students compared to all students, white and nonwhite, Southern and non-Southern. In Section II, on the survey of high school graduates entering college, we explained the difficulty of getting the test scores for this sample. We noted that we ended up with scores for about 70 per cent of the students.

On the Negro college student sample we fared even less well in our attempts to secure test scores. This was a considerable disappointment, since it was only for the college student sample that we could have related test-score ranking to the major background variables, such as education and occupation of parents, and family income.

Since national standing on test scores is presumably the best and most objective measure of a student's academic status, whether thought of as aptitude, preparation, or both at once, we shall describe the problems we encountered in trying to collect these data.

In the first place, the colleges found the clerical job of transcribing the scores for large aggregates of students a time-consuming one, and there were long delays in obtaining the returns for the forty-two colleges which eventually furnished them. We sent forms for the test-score data somewhat later than the student questionnaire, using the student questionnaires as a basis for indicating to each college those of their students for whom we needed scores. A large part of the telephone follow-up of the college survey was devoted to attempts to obtain test-score returns.

Purely apart from the problem of obtaining the data, where it was available, there was the general problem of missing data.

For the returns we did receive, there were hardly any scores for the considerable proportions of transfer students. In addition, several colleges indicated that the scores simply did not exist in the available records. In another college the records had been lost concurrent with a change in personnel responsible for testing. In several additional instances the only records were in the custody of the organization originating the test, and efforts to obtain them proved fruitless.

Since student scores on the most common test were ostensibly in the files of the organization originating the test, we hoped to obtain test data for over half the colleges from this file. Due to a variety of reasons the desired information could not be obtained.

In brief, after extended efforts we ended up with twenty-six colleges for which we had almost no test information. For the colleges which sent us data there were numerous lacunae, representing transfer students, plus large numbers of other students for whom the data were not available for unknown reasons. Hence, our final decision was that the information we obtained was far too incomplete to use.

V.   General Evaluation of the Surveys

We believe that the "recruitment" survey data are very reliable in all ways. Not only did we obtain a high response rate from the relevant universe of colleges, but also there was little

omission of items of information requested.
Finally, there is every evidence of care in
answering the questions.

   The two other surveys do not approach the
"recruitment" survey in reliability. For both,
sampling was more complex, the information sought
more difficult in many instances to supply, and
lacunae in responses to certain questions greater.
We believe, however, that the findings we present
in our study are more than sufficiently accurate
for deciding on policies and action programs.

APPENDIX C

NOTES ON COLLEGE QUALITY RATINGS

APPENDIX   C   NOTES ON
COLLEGE
QUALITY
RATINGS

INTRODUCTION

American colleges and universities have
usually been rated for over-all academic quality
in one of two ways. In some instances presumed
indicators of quality are used in combination,
such as the size of the library, size of faculty
salaries, proportion of faculty with advanced
degrees, student-teacher ratio, and so forth.
Another way involves obtaining evaluations of the
colleges from a number of experts, evaluations
based simply on broad familiarity with the
schools.

In this study we selected a quality rating of
the four-year primarily Negro colleges based on
the latter procedure. Since the universe of Negro
colleges is a relatively small one, and also a
unique one among all colleges, it seemed plausible
that an authority on these schools could make
reasonable value judgments about very nearly all
of them, insuring considerable relative uniformity
in the rating for the universe of schools by each
expert. In addition, objective indicators of
quality of colleges are far from precise, and this
imprecision can badly distort ratings when the
number of schools is small. Special situations

may make one or more of the indicators in a
quality index misleading. For example, faculty
salaries in public colleges vary with the economic
means of the locale of the college, and the consequent ratings of better colleges in a less affluent region may be undeservedly low as compared
with ratings of better colleges in a more affluent
region.

Before adopting the ratings made by experts
from their personal knowledge, we attempted to
test, to the extent possible, the comparative
validity of the two approaches. The quality of a
number of the primarily Negro colleges, relative
to the universe of these colleges, is almost uni-
versally recognized as being very high, and to
these schools we applied two existing rating
systems based on a number of presumed indicators
of academic excellence (size of library, student-
teacher ratio, etc.). Discrepancies between the
expected ratings and those deriving from the indicators were frequent, and we concluded that these
rating systems, while they might be generally
valid for all colleges in the country, were too
imprecise when applied to our small special universe.

On the other hand, the ratings by experts
conformed with the generally held evaluation of
these same schools, and we inferred that, with
their extensive knowledge of the less-known
schools, the experts' judgments would have over-
all validity. There is considerable internal and
inferential evidence on the credibility of their
decisions, but before we discuss this we will
speak of the ratings themselves.

ORIGINAL RATINGS BY EXPERTS

The ratings used in this study were developed
in the early 1960's by a well-known organization
concerned with higher education, for the express

purpose of planning an educational program. For this program it was necessary to know which of the Negro colleges were of sufficient quality to merit inclusion. The ratings were developed for a serious practical objective, and consequently were made with considerable care.

We were allowed to use these ratings on the understanding that the name of the organization originating them and of the experts who did the ratings, as well as the actual ratings of particular colleges and universities, would be held in confidence. However, we can describe the manner in which the ratings were made, the way in which we applied them to our data, and our efforts to check their validity.

Six experts on the primarily Negro colleges independently rated each of the colleges, and the final rating for each college was the arithmetic average of these independent ratings for the college. The assumption was that with a number of raters for each college, a biased rating by one particular rater or another would seldom alter the final quality category of a college.

The raters assigned scores from 0.0 to 3.0 to the colleges and were permitted to express their scores in quarters of the three one-point intervals—as 1.25, for example, or 2.50. Thus a rater, feeling modest doubt whether a college was really "good," could express this doubt, and frequently did so, by reducing the rating for that college by a quarter or a half a point, rather than expressing this doubt by the more drastic reduction of a full point. However, the final intervals we used to represent "good," "fair," and "poor" colleges were broader ones, as follows:

"Poor" colleges	"Fair" colleges	"Good" colleges
0.0 to 1.4	1.5 to 2.4	2.5 to 3.0

The advantage of using a three-category rating over a simple dichotomy was simply that it would tend to keep the two extremes--the "good" and the "poor" colleges, which were the most significant groups for comparison--relatively pure. Misrating might place a college which was in fact "poor" in the "fair" group, but there was far less likelihood of its being so misrated as to fall in the "good" group. By the same token, a college which was actually "good" would be most likely to be misrated "fair," and least likely to be "poor." The reader could, if he wished, ignore the "fair" group entirely, interpreting it as representing colleges which were difficult to rate, or possibly in the process of quality change.

An analysis of the extent of agreement in the ratings for the three quality groups tends to support such interpretation. For each of the three quality groups the proportions of all the separate rating decisions which agreed with the position in which the colleges finally fell were as follows:

"Poor" colleges	"Fair" colleges	"Good" colleges
78%	56%	74%

The raters were in quite close agreement as to which colleges were "good" ones and which were "poor" ones. They agreed less as to which ones were "fair." We conclude, then, that since the colleges of somewhat indeterminate quality, so far as the raters were concerned, fell principally in the middle group, our findings for "poor" and "good" colleges, the main concern, should be especially reliable.

The conclusions we reached appear even more reasonable when we consider the basis for rating the colleges in the three quality groups. "Poor" designated colleges where the raters felt that the academic offering was clearly deficient, and where

they saw little chance of substantial improvement
within five years. "Fair" colleges were ones
where the academic offering, though deficient,
might well improve substantially within five
years. "Good" colleges were simply what this
term denotes. The possibility of improvement
would seem to be the hardest question for the
raters to determine, and their comparatively high
incidence of disagreement as to which colleges
were "fair" ones probably reflects this difficulty.

This supposition is strengthened by the fact
that two thirds of the individual disagreements
with the final ratings of the "fair" colleges
would have placed the controversial colleges in
the "poor" group, presumably on the basis of
"poor" current quality, plus a deviant opinion on
the possibility of improvement. By and large,
then, one might view the "fair" group as being
more similar to the "poor" group than to the
"good" group, about which there was apparently
little disagreement, all evidence considered.

Not all raters felt able to rate every college, and we singled out for special consideration
colleges rated by three or less raters. There
were ten such colleges, eight of them rated by
three raters, and two by only two raters. In
these instances a single deviant rating could well
have placed a college in a different quality category. For each of these colleges we sought
supplementary opinions on the rating accorded it.
In no case did this alter the original rating.

There was a single instance where we
seriously questioned the rating of a college, and
we talked with other experts during the course of
the study who also questioned it. A single large
college rated as "fair" was felt to be as
plausibly, and perhaps more plausibly, a "good"
college. Because of the size of the college this
rating change could affect our final statistics

appreciably. It turned out, however, that placing this college in the "good" rather than the "fair" group would have simply increased the sizes of the differences we report. We decided to abide by the raters' decisions and err, if their rating was indeed in error, on the side of conservatism.

If the reader accepts the general credibility of the ratings, as we have described them, then we feel justified in maintaining that the findings by quality of college are real ones. We do not report as findings differences of a few percentage points, which might result from the admitted imprecision inherent in the ratings. The reader is free to ignore the middle group of "fair" colleges, as we have pointed out, but the findings by quality of college nevertheless remain.

1967 RATINGS

Early in 1967, after we had completed our tabulations and analysis by quality of college, a very recent, independently developed rating of the four-year primarily Negro colleges became available. This new rating presented four "tentative groupings of the Negro colleges," and was comparable in basic approach to our own quality index, though it differed slightly in the definition of the quality categories and in the total of colleges covered. Like the rating index we used, the new one represented expert personal judgment on the academic quality of colleges, rather than scores statistically determined from the presence or absence of specific "hardware" or "software" characteristics (faculty salaries, books per student, etc.) felt to be associated with academic quality.

The colleges were classified as:

   I. Top quality
  II. Next to top quality

III. Next to bottom quality

IV. Bottom quality (including those
       for which there was inadequate
       information)

The seventy-seven colleges for which we have
quality ratings from both sources are distributed
as follows:

| | Ratings as used in present study | | | | |
1967 Ratings	"Good"	"Fair"	"Poor"	Total	Av. score
I	7	1	--	8	2.7
II	7	7	1	15	2.3
III	4	12	4	20	1.8
IV	1	11	22	34	1.3
Total	19	31	27	77	--

There appear to be serious differences only for
six of the seventy-seven colleges. Five which we
considered as "good" were classified as III or IV,
next to or bottom quality. One which we considered as "poor" was rated as II or next to top
quality.

It is possible that the ratings are even more
comparable than the above cross-classification
suggests since the two ratings were made about
five years apart. During such a time period it is
possible for a college to change enough to move
from one to another category.

As a test of the general comparability of
findings for the two indexes we selected a tabulation of increase in new entrants to four-year

Negro colleges, 1962-1965, by quality of college--
since this particular tabulation is basic to many
of our conclusions. As the data on the following
page show, the two independent ratings give
similar results.

The chief difference in the two rating
schemes appears to be that the 1967 rating was
extremely selective with regard to inclusion in
Group I, its highest quality group. Only eight
colleges are included in this category, whereas
twenty colleges are "good" ones by the rating
scheme we used. This is partially the natural
effect of a four-category scheme as compared to a
three-category one. Nearly half of the Group II
colleges and about a fifth of the Group III colleges fell within our "good" category, representing about 6 in 20 of all new entrants, as compared with the 3 in 20 for Group I of the 1967
rating.

THE ELITE COLLEGES

The National Merit Scholarship Corporation
developed a rating of colleges based on the
schools which high ability students wished to
attend. Presumably those colleges which attract
the most able students are the best. Using the
data presented in College Preferences of Eleventh
Grade Students,* we determined for each Negro
college the proportion of all test participants
hoping to enter this college, who scored 95 or
better on the test. This procedure selected out
the following six colleges for which we had information about the characteristics of the students:

------

*College Preferences of Eleventh Grade Stu-
dents, NMSC Research Reports, Vol. 2, No. 9
(Evanston, Ill.: National Merit Scholarship Corporation, 1966).

Two Recent College Quality Indexes Compared for Relationship to Per Cent Increase in New Entrants, 1962-1965

Quality Index Used in This Study

	"Good" colleges (deserve this designation currently)	"Fair" colleges (not currently "good," but may become so in next five years)	"Poor" colleges (currently "poor," and show little prospect of improvement)	All colleges
	%	%	%	%
Per cent increase in new entrants, 1962-1965	-18	+20	+43	+25

N = 84 four-year colleges

Comparison Index – 1967 Ratings

	Group I (Clearly superior within population)	Group II (Institutions with promise)	Group III (Lesser quality)	Group IV (Lesser quality yet, & includes colleges about which information is lacking)	All Groups
Per cent increase in new entrants, 1962-1965	-3	+31	+35	+36	+27

N = 78 four-year colleges

Note: The slight difference in the over-all increase in new entrants for the two ratings is explained by six colleges included in one instance, and not included in the other.

Xavier University, Louisiana

Howard University, Washington, D.C.

Lincoln University, Pennsylvania

Fisk University, Tennessee

Morehouse College, Georgia

Hampton Institute, Virginia

There were two other colleges that should be considered as elite, Lincoln University, Missouri, and Central State College, Ohio, but we had no information about their student body. Of all the students who took the tests and specified one of these six colleges as their first choice, 24 per cent scored 95 or better. On the other hand, for the fifteen other primarily Negro colleges which we had classified as "good," an average of only 9 per cent of those who took the test and selected one of them scored 95 or better. Among the remaining colleges rated "fair" and "poor" according to our classification, only 3 per cent of those who took the test and selected one of them scored 95 or better. Omitted are about twenty-five colleges--primarily nonaccredited--which no one selected, or else were omitted from the list from which the students made their choices.

On the basis of the information which we collected from the Southern Negro high schools, we were able to test the NMSC list by noting the colleges which the students in the upper half of the test scores expected to attend in the Fall of 1965. These better students selected the same six elite colleges.

APPENDIX D

PAST AND PRESENT TEST PERFORMANCE

APPENDIX D PAST AND
PRESENT
TEST
PERFORMANCE

INTRODUCTION

In Chapter 2 we presented evidence that both
in 1940 and 1965 Southern Negro students performed
far less well than all students in the country,
white and nonwhite, on tests of ability and
achievement. Since this conclusion is critical
for the analysis, and since questions can be
raised about the statistical reliability of the
test-score data, we sought additional information.
Two types of supplementary evidence are available:

1) The Office of Education's 1964-1966
    study of Equality of Educational
    Opportunity in the United States
    provides systematic test-score data
    for the white majority group and a
    number of minority groups of school
    children in five elementary and
    secondary grades. Various tests
    were administered--verbal, nonverbal,
    general information, etc.--and the
    data were tabulated by region since
    the samples were large. Many of the
    findings may be directly compared
    with those of our study. Others,
    deriving from types of data our study

245

did not attempt to collect, extend
the implications of our own conclusions. We will summarize some
of the descriptive findings of this
study, and we refer the reader to
the full published report.[1]

2) Data for men tested by the U.S.
Armed Forces from the time of World
War I to the mid-1960's. These are
available by color and by region,
and offer evidence regarding the
generality of our test-score findings
for Southern Negro high school
seniors.

SOME FINDINGS OF THE
OFFICE OF EDUCATION STUDY

Wherever the two studies can be compared, the
findings are essentially the same. In both instances, Southern Negro twelfth graders performed
relatively poorly.

For our study the comparison is a relatively
broad one between seniors in Southern Negro high
schools, the great majority of all Southern Negro
seniors, and all students in the country, white
and nonwhite. The Office of Education study, however, compares all Southern Negro twelfth graders
with Southern white twelfth graders, and with white
and nonwhite twelfth graders in the Northeast, the
Midwest, the West, and the Southwest.[2] In
addition, it offers comparisons with all Mexican
Americans, all Puerto Rican Americans, all Indian
Americans, and all Oriental Americans. Comparisons are offered for first, third, sixth, and
ninth graders, in addition to twelfth graders or
high school seniors. The study presents comparisons for a number of different types of tests
separately--verbal ability, nonverbal ability,
reading comprehension, mathematics achievement,

and general information in three areas, practical
arts, social sciences, and humanities--as well as
the general information total. A wider variety of
tests was given to older than to younger pupils,
since some of these tests only become relevant
with greater maturity. What were the essential
findings?

First, let us consider the twelfth graders,
equivalent to the high school seniors in our
study. Southern and Southwestern Negro students
did considerably less well on all the various
tests than all other regional and racial groups
tested. The only exceptions to this rule are instances on several of the tests in which Puerto
Rican or Mexican Americans did as poorly or
slightly more so. The other two minorities,
Indian Americans and Oriental Americans, and
especially the latter, did considerably better
than Southern Negro youth. No matter what the
region, the white majority group placed far higher
than did the Southern Negro. This is true even
when the Southern Negro youth are compared with
Southern white youth, the regional group of white
seniors which placed lowest.

Furthermore, of all the Negro regional
groups, the Southern Negro seniors fared least
well on these tests. Quite clearly, they are an
especially disadvantaged group, if such tests are
the measure of educational disadvantage. It
should be noted, however, that Negro youth from
other regions, though they placed higher than
Negroes from the South, also performed very
poorly as compared with all regional groups of
white students. In other words, we can say that
the very poor test performance of Southern Negro
seniors is simply the most extreme instance of
relative educational deprivation which applies to
Negro youth throughout the country.

It is also true that the differences between
the Negro and white groups, including the Southern

Negro youth, decrease at successively lower grades. Apparently, and very significantly, the relative educational deprivation for Negro youth is a cumulative one over the years of primary and secondary schooling. It is greatest as the Negro youth approaches college age.

Let us illustrate the increasing differences in test-score performance with increasing age, between the Negro minority and the white majority. (The statistics which follow are for the national aggregates of both groups of students, and the differences would be somewhat greater if Southern Negro youth alone were tabulated.)

Nationwide Median Test Scores for First and Twelfth Grade Pupils, Fall, 1965

Test	Racial or Ethnic Group		
	Negro	Majority	Difference
First grade:			
Nonverbal	43.4	54.1	10.7
Verbal	45.4	53.2	7.8
Twelfth grade:			
Nonverbal	40.9	52.0	11.1
Verbal	40.9	52.1	11.2
Average of five tests*	41.1	52.0	10.9

Source: James S. Coleman, et al., Equality of Educational Opportunity (Washington, D.C.: U.S. Office of Education, 1966).

*The five tests (nonverbal, verbal, reading, mathematics, and general information) are available only for the twelfth graders.

In order to interpret the findings, it is
necessary to know that the "scores on each test at
each grade level were standardized so that the
average over the national sample equaled 50 and
the standard deviation equaled 10. This means
that for all pupils in the nation, about 16 percent would score below 40 and about 16 percent
above 60."[3] Because of the mode of statistical
presentation, at first glance the numerical differences might suggest slighter actual differences
between the two groups than if, for example, the
two groups had been tabulated according to their
national quartile test distribution, or if the
Negro student performance had been expressed in
years of grade retardation. With this fact in
mind, the increase in the differences between the
Negro and the white majority pupils between the
first and the twelfth grades is a substantial one,
and most clearly so in the case of the "verbal"
testing.

There is one discrepancy between the Office
of Education findings on the academic level of
achievement of Negro twelfth graders and the
findings from our study. From the former it would
appear that under 15 per cent of Southern Negro
youth performed as well as the average white student. Our data indicate a higher proportion, in
the neighborhood of 25 per cent. The chief reason
for this difference is that the Office of Education study administered tests to *all* twelfth
graders, whereas we obtained information only on
twelfth graders *planning on college,* and who had
been tested as well. The college planners were an
academically superior group in their classes. Of
the 3 in 10 students planning on college, three
quarters were in the top half of the class
ranking. Less than half of the 7 in 10 not
planning on college would be in that group. In
addition, some of the college planners had never
taken tests, and these students, perforce omitted
from our test statistics, appear to be the less
able college candidates planning on poorer Negro

colleges, or two-year colleges, which generally do
not require tests from their applicants. In
brief, though the college planners apparently are
considerably more able than all Southern Negro
high school seniors, still only about a quarter of
them appear to equal the performance of the
average student tested throughout the country.

Presumably, the level of preparation of Negro
high school seniors compared to that of white
seniors, as evidenced in these statistics, should
make it difficult for Negro youth to obtain admission to colleges not specifically concerned
with remedial programs in the first years. The
problem should be especially acute if admission to
higher quality colleges were in question.

ARMED FORCES TESTS

The Armed Forces test results show that the
poor relative performance of the Southern Negro
students in 1940 and 1965 is simply a specific
instance of the more general finding that Negroes,
down the years, have consistently, and to a marked
degree, ranked low on such tests.

Both whites and Negroes apparently performed
somewhat better at the time of World War II than
during World War I, but it is impossible to say
with any certainty whether there was any significant decrease in the differences between the test
performances of the two groups. The populations
compared over the years have not been identical,
and the tests have differed considerably. Only
the broadest comparisons may be made. We can say
that if Negroes did in fact improve their test
performance relative to whites, as some writers
maintain, very large differences remain today.
The magnitudes of these current differences
strongly suggest that Negroes will continue to
perform substantially less well than whites in the
foreseeable future, unless new and potent forces
are brought to bear upon the problem.[4]

World War I

During the first World War soldiers were tested on the Alpha, Beta, and several other tests. Brigham has presented data for Negroes and whites for the combined tests, and from these data we can derive the fact that just under 1 in 6 Negroes ranked in the upper half of the distribution for both races combined.[5] Southern Negroes ranked very significantly below Northern Negroes, and this was also true for Southern, as compared to Northern, whites.

Within each region, however, Negroes ranked well below whites, and the difference was largest in the South. The extent of regional differences at the time of World War I may be seen from the following table (showing average scores of recruits in 1918):[6]

Region	Recruits	
	Negro	White
	(group average)	
Southern	9.8	12.7
Northern	12.0	14.1

Northern Negroes performed very nearly as well as Southern whites, though considerably less well than Northern whites.

Draftees, 1964-1965

The test scores obtained from preinduction examination of draftees in the period 1964-1965 reveal substantially the same story. The white draftees scored considerably higher than did the Negroes. Both white and Negro draftees from the

South performed below the national average. But
the Southern Negroes performed most poorly of all.
These ethnic and regional differences persist even
when formal educational attainment is taken into
account.[7]

The proportions who failed the mental tests
were as follows:

	White %	Negro %
Failed mental tests		
Total United States	14.5	59.3
South	20.3	66.5
Failed mental tests and medically disqualified		
Total United States	1.5	4.3
South	2.1	4.7

Of the draftees who did pass the mental tests
the following proportions were found in the upper
35 per cent of the standard population, i.e., the
relatively high scorers:

	White %	Negro %
Total United States	45.1	7.9
South	35.5	4.6

Whatever derogatory remarks may be ventured
about the significance of these tests of ability

and achievement, one important and indisputable
fact remains. These tests do measure the ability
to do high grade college and professional work.
Accordingly, a person who does poorly on these
tests is very likely to have trouble getting high
grades in college, or even entering college, and
in carrying on high quality professional work
(i.e., "high quality" as evaluated by his professional peers).

NOTES TO APPENDIX D

1. James S. Coleman, et al., Equality of
Educational Opportunity (Washington, D.C.: U.S.
Office of Education, 1966). See especially
section 3.0, "Pupil Achievement and Motivation."

2. The Office of Education study and our
study differ slightly in the classification of
states into regional groups. Precise comparisons,
then, are not possible, but the differences are
not such as to affect the general conclusions we
reach. The differences are as follows:

1) The Office of Education study has
    a regional category, "Southwest,"
    which includes Texas and Oklahoma,
    both placed in our major category,
    "South," and in our sub-categories,
    "Other South" and "Border States,"
    respectively. The two other "South-
    west" states are Arizona and New
    Mexico, not entering into our
    analysis at all.

2) In the Office of Education study the
    states of Delaware and Maryland, and
    the District of Columbia, are placed
    in "Northeast." In our study they
    are in the "Border States."

NEGRO HIGHER EDUCATION IN THE 1960'S

The remaining fourteen states in the "South" in
our study are all included in the Office of Education study category of "South," and there are no
additional states in "South" in the latter study.

3. Coleman, op. cit., p. 20.

4. For a discussion of these gains in apti-
tude or achievement, relative to socio-economic
gains over the years, see: Howard Hale Long,
"The Relative Learning Capacities of Negroes and
Whites," Journal of Negro Education, Vol. XXVI,
No. 2, Spring, 1957, pp. 129-31.

5. H. E. Garrett, "Comparison of Negro and
White Recruits on the Army Tests Given in 1917-
1918," American Journal of Psychology, Vol. 58,
1945, p. 490.

6. Thelma G. Alper and E. G. Boring, "In-
telligence Test Scores of Northern and Southern
White and Negro Recruits in 1918," Journal of
Abnormal Social Psychology, Vol. 39, 1944, p. 472.

7. Bernard D. Karpinos, "The Mental Test
Qualification of American Youths for Military
Service and Its Relationship to Educational
Attainment," Proceedings of the Social Statistics
Section, American Statistical Association,
Washington, D.C., 1966, pp. 92ff.

APPENDIX E

PROJECTED EDUCATIONAL ATTAINMENT
OF SOUTHERN NEGRO YOUTH

APPENDIX   E   PROJECTED
EDUCATIONAL
ATTAINMENT
OF SOUTHERN
NEGRO YOUTH

FINDINGS

In 1960 Southern nonwhite (almost all Negro) youth aged eighteen to twenty-four had completed an average (median) of 10.5 years of schooling. By 1975 this average may increase to a little over 12 years. It is thought that perhaps half of the youth will have graduated from high school.

The 1975 estimated distribution by years of schooling completed for youth aged eighteen to twenty-four is shown in Table E.1.[1] The *high* estimate assumes that maximum proportions will finish high school and enter college. The *low* estimate assumes that the proportions attending school in 1975 will be substantially similar to those observed in 1960; i.e., that there would be no increase. The *medium* estimate assumes moderate increases in school attendance.

Table E.1

Distribution of years of schooling completed, of Southern nonwhite youth aged eighteen to twenty-four, 1960 and projected 1975 estimates

Years of schooling completed	Numbers (in thousands)				Percentage distribution			
	Actual 1960	Projected 1975			Actual 1960	Projected 1975		
		High	Medium	Low		High	Medium	Low
TOTAL	1065	1915	1915	1915	100.0	100.0	100.0	100.0
0 to 8 years	339	65	337	611	31.9	3.4	17.6	31.9
9 to 11 years	388	810	767	696	36.4	42.3	40.0	36.4
12 years	247	722	593	468	23.2	37.7	31.0	24.4
13+ years	91	318	218	140	8.5	16.6	11.4	7.3
Median years	10.5	12.1	11.4	10.5	--	--	--	--

Based on data shown in Table E.2.

We think that the *high* estimate is quite
reasonable. If this should be correct, it will
mean that almost everyone will at least have
finished elementary school; over half who will
have entered high school will graduate; perhaps
a third of the high school graduates will have
finished at least one year of college. Probably
more than one third of the high school graduates
eventually will enter college, although many of
them may be twenty-five years of age or over.

An increase in the numbers of youth aged
eighteen to twenty-four will, by itself, result
in at least a doubling of the numbers attending
college (Chart E.1). There were about 1 million
youth in this age group in 1960, and it is thought
that there may be almost 2 million in 1975. Un-
expected high migration out of the South could, of
course, reduce this number significantly.

SOME IMPLICATIONS

1) Population increase alone would very
nearly double the number of Southern Negro high
school graduates between the years 1960 and 1975.
Even if we assume that both the proportion of the
relevant age group entering high school, and the
proportion of the entrants completing high school,
remain the same in 1975 as in 1960--in defiance of
clear trends, 1940-1960--substantial increases in
college facilities would be indicated.

2) The more likely possibility, in our
opinion, is that past trends which have led to
substantial increases in proportions entering and
graduating from high school, 1940-1960, quite
apart from population changes, will continue
through 1975. Our medium estimate for 1975
assumes that there will be some moderation of the
rate of increase as the age group approaches total
attendance at a given educational level. Our high

Chart E.1

Southern Nonwhite Population Eighteen to
Twenty-Four Years of Age, 1940–1960, and
Projected for 1975[a]

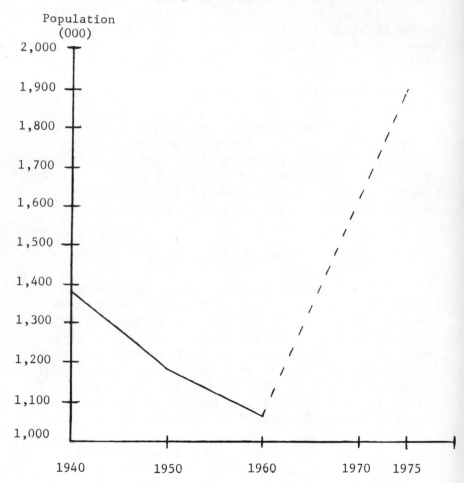

[a]Thirteen states and the District of Columbia;
each had a total nonwhite population of
250,000 or more in 1960.

Source: U.S. Bureau of the Census, Current
Population Reports, Series P-25,
No. 326, February 7, 1966, Table 7.

estimate assumes that the rate of increase will
continue largely unchanged. On the first
assumption there would be just under two and one
half times the 1960 high school graduates by 1975,
and on the second assumption slightly over three
times the number. In either eventuality, very
large increases in college facilities for Southern
Negro high school graduates would be necessary, if
the 1960 college-going rate were merely to be
maintained.

3) The college-going rate of Southern Negro
high school graduates rose about 3.5 per cent
between 1940 and 1950, and then dropped about 8.5
per cent between 1950 and 1960--in other words,
declining about 5 per cent in the twenty-year
span. We may reasonably assume that the opportunities afforded by the G.I. Bill were major de-
terminants of the 1950 gain. For the 1960 decline
we might hypothesize that the 1950-1960 increment
to the proportion of the age group completing high
school included many students for whom a secondary
education was a new, and also a terminal, educational goal. Entering college is a decision of a
different order from that of completing lower
levels of schooling within a completely separate
and expense-free public system. We can only
speculate whether the terminal goal for many high
school students is now shifting from high school
graduation to at least some college experience.
The new G.I. Bill, the Federal student loan program, the Federal work-study program, continuing
growth of the public two-year college, and emphasis on the value of college in a technologically
changing economy may presage such a shift, and
well may reverse the 1940-1960 trend in rates of
college entrance. From the evidence we cannot
predict what will in fact occur, but only note
that if increased facilities and increased mone-
tary assistance were available in the next few
years, it would seem reasonable that Negro high

school graduates would increasingly avail themselves of them, especially if the presumed advantages of college are emphasized.

If the 1940-1960 decline were to continue
through 1975, the increment to college entrants
1960-1975 would be a modest 54 per cent. If the
past trend reversed itself the increment would be
a very large one of about 250 per cent. If the
1960 rate of college entrance by Southern Negro
high school graduates were to pertain in 1975, the
increment would be about 140 per cent, implying
large expansion over current college facilities.
Generally we favor this latter possibility.

Our three projections of college entrance
chiefly illustrate, then, the very broad range of
demand for college facilities for Southern Negro
high school graduates that is possible in 1975--
a range in considerable measure determined by the
actions of educators and government.

METHODOLOGY OF THE PROJECTIONS

Sources of Data

Our two basic data sources for the projections were the education volumes of the 1940,
1950, and 1960 U.S. Censuses of Population, and
Current Population Reports, "Population Estimates," Series P-25, No. 326, February, 1966.
From the former we were able to establish the
relevant population at each of the three dates
and the number who had at least entered high
school, at least completed high school, and who
had at least some post-high school education. The
measure of educational attainment was the standard
Census one: number of years of schooling completed. The relevant population was Southern

Negroes between the ages of eighteen and twenty-
four. We use this age cohort as an approximation
of the total of potential college entrants at any
given date. Few students enter college prior to
eighteen, and few enter past the mid-twenties. It
is true, however, that Negroes, as compared to
whites, are more frequently late entrants to college. In any case, our choice of this age group
was dictated by necessity, since it was the only
one suited to our purposes tabulated for all three
Censuses and the Current Population Reports as
well.

The Current Population Reports permitted us
to extend the 1940, 1950, and 1960 Southern Negro
population figures for the relevant age group to
1975. Two 1975 population projection figures
(nonwhites aged eighteen to twenty-four in the
Southern states) were presented in the Current
Population Reports, based on alternative assumptions regarding fertility and net migration. The
two figures differed so little, however (1,897,000
versus 1,932,000), that we felt quite justified in
simplifying procedures by using an average of the
two alternatives. The average departs less than
1 per cent from either of the two figures.

General Procedures

In developing the projections of educational
attainment, 1975, we simply applied the known
trends in educational attainment, 1940-1960, to
the projected population, 1975. We first established changes in the proportions of the total
population entering high school 1940-1960. We
then established changes in the proportions of
these entrants graduating from high school. We
finally established changes in the proportions of
the high school graduates completing at least a
year of college. The number and proportion of the

1975 Southern nonwhite population graduating from
high school depended, for example, on two trends,
1940-1960: 1) the trend in high school entrance
for the relevant population, and 2) the trend in
high school graduation for these entrants. We
projected the two historical trends for the two
levels of attainment three different ways,
yielding high, low, and medium figures, representing optimistic and pessimistic estimates, plus
a compromise between these two extremes. The same
procedure was followed at the college attendance
level.

The two extreme figures, then, define the
range of possibilities, whereas the third figure
is the statistical middle of this range. We
emphasize that this third figure is simply a
statistical artifact, since a judgment based on
evaluation of probabilities in regard to educational policy and practice over the next few years
could well depart from this statistical average.

The final projections are shown in Table E.2.

Projecting Numbers of High School Entrants

For high school entrants our low estimate is
based on the assumption that the proportion of the
relevant population entering high school in 1960
remains the same in 1975. Our high estimate
assumes that the large 1940-1960 increase continues to the point where practically all of the
population enters by 1975. The increase could not
continue to that date at the historical rate, however, since this would mean that more than 100 per
cent of the population would have entered high
school in 1975, so we arbitrarily chose 96.6 per
cent as the terminal rate, the 1961 entrance rate
for white children nationally. Our medium estimate is the statistical average of the two extremes (Chart E.2).

Chart E.2

Number of Southern Nonwhite Youth Eighteen
to Twenty-Four Years of Age Who Completed
at Least the First Year of High School,
1940-1960, and Projected for 1975

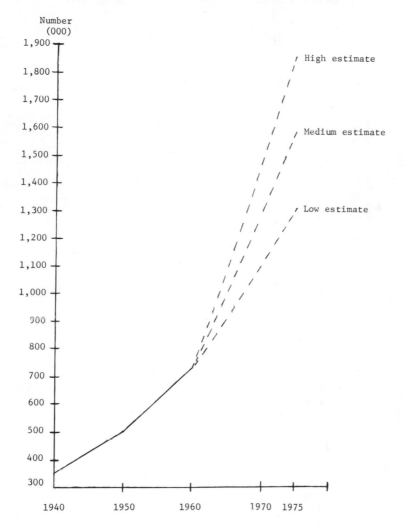

Source: Derived from data in the U.S. Census of
Population, 1940, 1950, and 1960. For
further explanations, see the text of
this appendix.

Table E.2

Methodology for making 1975 projections of educational attainment of Southern nonwhite youth aged eighteen to twenty-four

Year	Population 18 to 24 years (in thousands) (a)	% who had entered high school (b)	No. who had entered high school (in thousands)	% of high school entrants who graduated from high school (c)	No. who graduated from high school (in thousands)	% of high school graduates who finished one year of college (d)	No. who finished one year of college
Actual							
1940	1,365	25.5	348	37.5	130	31.8	42
1950	1,176	42.0	494	40.2	199	35.2	70
1960	1,065	68.1	726	46.6	338	26.8	91
Projected 1975							
High	1,915	96.6	1,850	56.2	1,040	30.6	318
Medium	1,915	82.4	1,578	51.4	811	26.8	218
Low	1,915	68.1	1,304	46.6	608	23.1	140

Notes for Table E.2

(a) Population figures derived from: U.S. Bureau of the Census. U.S. Census of Population: 1940. "Educational Attainment by Economic Characteristics and Marital Status," Table 2; U.S. Census of Population: 1950. "Education," Table 5; U.S. Census of Population: 1960. "Educational Attainment," Table 2 (Washington, D.C.: U.S. Government Printing Office, 1947, 1953, 1963). High school entrants from same sources. High school graduates and college entrants from same sources.

Projected 1975 population derived from Current Population Report of the Census Bureau, "Illustrative Projections of the Population of States: 1970 to 1985" (Series P-25, No. 326, February 7, 1966), Table 7. The projected 1975 population is the average of the two figures given for thirteen states, plus the District of Columbia (1897 + 1932 ÷ 2).

(b) Each of the three percentages is applied to the 1975 population estimate to yield: (1) a high projection of high school entrants, 96.6 per cent of the estimated 1975 population, the 1961 national rate for all white children in the 18-19 year age cohort; (2) a low estimate, 68.1 per cent of the population, the 1960 rate of entrance for Southern Negro children; and (3) a medium estimate midway between the high and the low estimates.

(c) The high percentage assumes continuation of the 1950-1960 intercensal increase in entrants who graduated, the greatest of the two intercensal increases. The low percentage assumes that the 1960 rate would pertain in 1975. The medium percentage was the average of the high and the low.

(d) The high percentage assumes a reversal of the 1940-1960 entrance drop. The low percentage assumes a continuation of the 1940-1960 drop to 1975. The medium percentage assumes that the 1960 rate pertains in 1975.

267

Projecting Numbers of
High School Graduates

The historical change in proportions of high
school entrants graduating from high school represents a consistent increase, 1940-1960. This increase, however, is a relatively slight one, when
compared to the rise in high school entrants over
the two decades. Our low projection of high
school graduates is based on a continuation to
1975 of the 1960 rate. Our high estimate assumes
that the 1950-1960 increase, the sharpest of the
two intercensal changes, pertains for the period
1960-1975. Our medium projection is the statistical average of the two extremes (Chart E.3).

A previous study of ours traced the educational attainment of all nonwhites in this
country for very nearly a hundred years, and
found that there was a slight long-term decline
in proportions of entrants graduating from high
school.[2] We attribute the rise we have found for
Southern Negro children to the low base level of
attainment of this group, as compared to Negroes
in other parts of the country. We assume that
they have been simply "catching up" in the 1940-
1960 period.

Projections of Numbers Completing
at Least One Year of College

Historically, the proportion of Southern
Negro high school graduates entering college has
had no clear trend. The proportion rose between
1940 and 1950, and then dropped a few points
below the 1940 level by 1960. For the subsequent
drop there is no clear explanation. The drop con-
trasts with a relatively constant proportion for
white children over a long historical span.[3] Our
assumption for the low projection of college entrants disregards the 1950 rise, and simply

Chart E.3

Number of Southern Nonwhite Youth Eighteen
to Twenty-Four Years of Age Who Completed
High School or More, 1940-1960, and
Projected for 1975

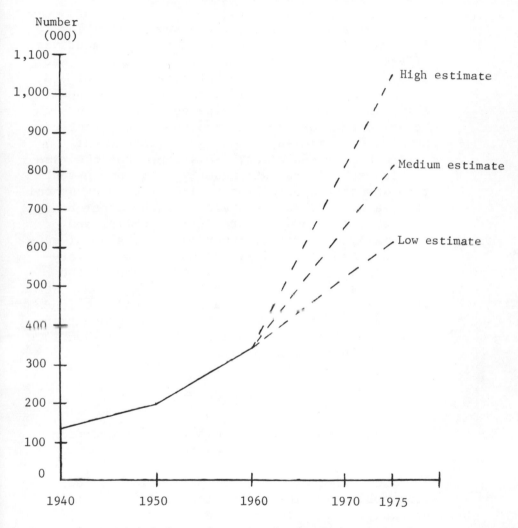

assumes that the 1940-1960 drop continues to 1975.
Our medium estimate is that the 1960 rate pertains
in 1975, and our high projection assumes a reversal
of the 1940-1960 trend in the period 1960-1975
(Chart E.4).

The rationale for these assumptions is as
follows: If there are no increases in incentives
offered Negro children for higher education, such
as G. I. Bills or other substantial forms of aid,
the historical drop could well continue--especi-
ally since the large anticipated increase in high
school graduates probably represents substantial
numbers of children with no great commitment
toward higher education. We assume that the rise
in high school graduation derives to some extent
from stricter application of laws regarding school
attendance until a given age. On the other hand,
strong feeling on the part of the public, and
especially of parents, regarding the value of education in an increasingly technological society--
especially if backed by substantial aid at the
college level--could well reverse the trend. We
are thinking of such innovations as college funds
assured students prior to high school graduation.
A balance of the factors could leave the 1960 rate
virtually unchanged in 1975.

SUMMARY

We may summarize our own guesses regarding
the alternate projections as follows:

We feel that stricter application of laws,
plus public sentiment favoring education, will
probably combine to increase the proportion of
Southern Negro children entering high school to
the point where it approximates that of white
children, or very nearly 100 per cent. We feel
that the same influences will operate to increase

Chart E.4

Number of Southern Nonwhite Youth Eighteen
to Twenty-Four Years of Age Who Completed
at Least the First Year of College,
1940-1960, and Projected for 1975

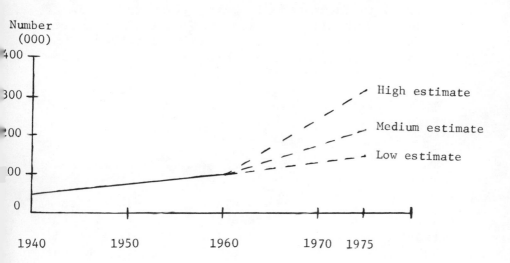

Source: Derived from data in the U.S. Census of
          Population, 1940, 1950, and 1960. For
          further explanations, see the text of
          this appendix.

the proportions graduating from high school,
though we also feel that the rise will be more
gradual. We feel that the 1960 college-going rate
will increase, since liberalized access to college
will in all probability persist, or even increase,
in the immediate future, and since the value of
college in later life is being given increasing
attention in all communications media. In short,
we feel that the strongest possibility is that
both the number of high school graduates, and the
number of persons with at least some college, in
the eighteen to twenty-four year age group in
1975, will be between two and three times the 1960
figures.

NOTES TO APPENDIX E

1. The numbers shown in this table differ
very slightly from those shown in Chapter 9. This
results from the fact that the projections in
Table E.1 were made for the entire South, whereas
those shown in Chapter 9 were made on a state-by-
state basis. The differences, however, are slight
and are within the margin of error of the basic
data.

2. A. J. Jaffe and Walter Adams, "Trends in
College Enrollment," College Board Review, Winter,
1964-65, No. 55, pp. 27ff.

3. Ibid.

APPENDIX F

SURVEY QUESTIONNAIRES

The College Entrance Examination Board and the Bureau of Applied Social Research of Columbia University, with the aid of the Fund for the Advancement of Education of the Ford Foundation, are jointly engaged in a study of the background characteristics of students enrolled in college this Fall. With ever increasing numbers of students going to college, it becomes ever more important to know who they are.

You are one of the students in our study. Please fill out and return this sheet with your other registration papers. The information you give will be used only for compilation of statistics; no information will be revealed about you or your college.

The success of this study depends on your cooperation. Will you please help?

```
1          2   3   4   5        6   7   8        9   10        11
[ ]      [ | | | ]        [ | | ]        [ | ]        [ ]
```

PLEASE ANSWER THE FOLLOWING QUESTIONS ON THE LINES PROVIDED, OR CHECK THE APPROPRIATE BOXES. IGNORE THE BOXES IMMEDIATELY ABOVE, AS WELL AS THE NUMBER NEXT TO THE ANSWERS BELOW.

Questions About You

1. YOUR NAME _____   2. SEX: 12–0 ☐ Male
   (Last)   (First)   (Middle Initial)   –1 ☐ Female

3. RACE: 13–0 ☐ Negro   4. AGE: 14–0 ☐ 18 years or less   –4 ☐ 22 years
          –1 ☐ White   –1 ☐ 19   "   –5 ☐ 23 or 24
          –2 ☐ Other   –2 ☐ 20   "   –6 ☐ 25 thru 29
                                     –3 ☐ 21   "   –7 ☐ 30 or over

5. YOUR MARITAL STATUS: 15–0 ☐ Never married   6. IN WHAT STATE WERE YOU BORN?
                         –1 ☐ Married, living   _____ ☐ ☐
                              with spouse   (Enter country,   16 17
                         –2 ☐ Other   if foreign born)

7. WHERE DO YOU LIVE WHILE ATTENDING COLLEGE?
   18–0 ☐ In a college dormitory or other residence connected with the college
    –1 ☐ In an apartment, hotel, or rooming house not connected with the college
    –2 ☐ At home with your family
    –3 ☐ With other relatives or friends

8. WHAT IS THE NAME AND LOCATION OF THE HIGH SCHOOL FROM WHICH YOU GRADUATED?

   _____   _____ ☐ ☐
           (Name)   (City or Town)   (State) 19 20

9. WHAT WAS YOUR HIGH SCHOOL COURSE OF STUDY?   21–0 ☐ College preparatory
                                                  –1 ☐ Not college preparatory

10. WHERE DID YOU STAND IN YOUR HIGH SCHOOL GRADUATION CLASS?
    22–0 ☐ Top quarter   –2 ☐ Third or bottom quarter
     –1 ☐ Second quarter   –3 ☐ Don't know

Questions About Your Family

11. WHO IS THE HEAD OF YOUR HOUSEHOLD?
    23–0 ☐ I am the head   –3 ☐ Other relative
     –1 ☐ My father   –4 ☐ Other non-relative
     –2 ☐ My mother

12. WHAT WAS YOUR FATHER'S AND YOUR MOTHER'S EDUCATION?
    Father   Mother
    24–0 ☐   25–0 ☐ Less than grammar school graduate
     –1 ☐   –1 ☐ Grammar school graduate
     –2 ☐   –2 ☐ Some high school
     –3 ☐   –3 ☐ High school graduate
     –4 ☐   –4 ☐ Post-high school technical or vocational training, but no college
     –5 ☐   –5 ☐ Some college
     –6 ☐   –6 ☐ College graduate
     –7 ☐   –7 ☐ Graduate or professional school

(OVER)

275

13. THE FOLLOWING QUESTIONS ARE ABOUT THE OCCUPATIONS OF YOUR FATHER AND MOTHER. BY OCCUPATION WE MEAN THE SPECIFIC KIND OF WORK DONE. FOR EXAMPLE, GOOD ANSWERS WOULD BE; "SOCIAL WORKER, GOVERNMENT AGENCY," OR "TEACHER, PUBLIC GRAMMAR SCHOOL," OR "FARMER, OWN FARM," OR "MACHINE OPERATOR, AUTO PARTS MANUFACTURE." IF YOU DO NOT KNOW THE OCCUPATION, WRITE IN "DON'T KNOW."

a. WHAT IS YOUR FATHER'S OCCUPATION? IF RETIRED, ENTER HIS LAST OCCUPATION.

_____ □ □ □
26 27 28

b. WHAT IS YOUR MOTHER'S OCCUPATION?

_____ Housewife only □   □ □ □
29 30 31

14. PLEASE ESTIMATE THE APPROXIMATE TOTAL YEARLY INCOME OF ALL PERSONS IN YOUR IMMEDIATE HOUSEHOLD. WE MEAN THE PERSONS WITH WHOM YOU LIVE WHEN YOU ARE NOT AWAY AT COLLEGE OR TRAVELING, PLUS YOU YOURSELF.

32–0 □ Under $2,000   –3 □ $4,000–4,999   –6 □ $8,000–9,999
   –1 □ $2,000–2,999   –4 □ $5,000–5,999   –7 □ $10,000 or more
   –2 □ $3,000–3,999   –5 □ $6,000–7,999   –8 □ Don't know

Questions About Your College Career

15. WHO WAS THE PERSON WHO ENCOURAGED YOU THE MOST TO GO TO COLLEGE?

33–0 □ No one in particular   –5 □ High school principal
   –1 □ Mother   –6 □ Minister or other church-related person
   –2 □ Father   –7 □ A prominent person in my home community
   –3 □ Other relative   –8 □ Someone connected with this college
   –4 □ High school teacher   9 □ Other person

16. WHAT ARE YOUR MAIN SOURCES OF FUNDS FOR MEETING COLLEGE EXPENSES?   □
CHECK AS MANY ANSWERS AS APPLY.   34

35–0 □ My immediate family contributes money
   –1 □ I have a scholarship, or other financial aid from the college
   –2 □ I have a government loan
   –3 □ I receive aid from a group not connected with the college
   –4 □ I use my personal savings
   –5 □ I work during the school year
   –6 □ I work during the Summer vacation
   –7 □ Other sources of funds _____
                                          (Please identify)

17. ARE YOU A FULL-TIME OR A PART-TIME STUDENT?   36–0 □ Full-time
                                                        –1 □ Part-time

18. IN WHAT YEAR OF COLLEGE ARE YOU ENROLLED THIS FALL?

37–0 □ Freshman   –2 □ Junior
   –1 □ Sophomore   –3 □ Senior

19. ARE YOU A DEGREE-CREDIT STUDENT? THAT IS, ARE YOU OFFICIALLY WORKING TOWARDS A RECOGNIZED ACADEMIC DEGREE, SUCH AS THE ASSOCIATE OF ARTS, OR THE BACHELOR OF ARTS OR OF SCIENCES?   38–0 □ Yes
                                                                    –1 □ No

20. WHAT IS YOUR MAJOR IN COLLEGE? IF YOU DO NOT YET HAVE A MAJOR, WHAT DO YOU THINK IT WILL BE?
Major_____or Expected Major _____ □ □
                                                        39 40

21. WHAT OCCUPATION DO YOU HOPE TO ENTER WHEN YOU FINISH YOUR EDUCATION? PLEASE IDENTIFY THE OCCUPATION SPECIFICALLY. FOR EXAMPLE, GOOD ANSWERS WOULD BE: "SALESMAN IN LIFE INSURANCE," OR "HISTORY TEACHER IN A COLLEGE," OR "LAWYER IN PRIVATE PRACTICE," OR "NON-EMPLOYED HOUSEWIFE."

_____ □ □ □
41 42 43

22. DO YOU PLAN TO ATTEND GRADUATE OR PROFESSIONAL SCHOOL?   44–0 □ Yes
                                                                  –1 □ No

23. IN WHAT PART OF THE COUNTRY DO YOU HOPE TO LIVE WHEN YOU FINISH YOUR EDUCATION?

45–0 □ The Western or Mountain states
   –1 □ The North Central states
   –2 □ The Southern or South Central states
   –3 □ The Northeastern or Middle Atlantic states
   –4 □ Outside the continental United States _____
                                          (Please identify country)

276

COLUMBIA UNIVERSITY IN THE CITY OF NEW YORK

Bureau of Applied Social Research

New York, N. Y.   10025

Winter, 1965-1966

1 ☐   2 ☐ 3 ☐ 4 ☐   5 ☐ 6 ☐   7 ☐ 8 ☐

PLEASE ANSWER THE FOLLOWING QUESTIONS ON THE LINES PROVIDED, OR CHECK THE APPROPRIATE BOXES.
IGNORE THE BOXES IMMEDIATELY ABOVE, AS WELL AS THE NUMBERS NEXT TO THE BOXES ABOVE AND BELOW.

Name of your college or university _____

Location _____   _____
          (Town or city)   (State)

Your title _____

QUESTIONS ABOUT STUDENT ENROLLMENT AND FINANCIAL AID

1. a. About how many degree-credit undergraduates were enrolled in your college . . .

         . . . in Fall, 1962?   . . . in Fall, 1965?

         9- _____   10- _____
              (Number)   (Number)

    b. About how many degree-credit undergraduates do you think will enroll in Fall, 1968?

         11- _____
              (Number)

2. We wish to ask you a few questions on (a) numbers of applicants, (b) numbers accepted,
    and (c) numbers actually enrolling. We are referring to degree-credit undergraduates only.

    a. About how many new applicants did your college have for the Fall of:

         1962 _____ 12-   1965 _____ 13-
                   (Number)   (Number)

    b. About how many of these applicants did your college accept for the Fall of:

         1962 _____ 14-   1965 _____ 15-
                   (Number)   (Number)

    c. About how many of the applicants who were accepted actually enrolled in the Fall of:

         1962 _____ 16-   1965 _____ 17-
                   (Number)   (Number)

              *   *   *   *   *   *   *   *   *   *   *

3. We would also like to ask you some questions on financial assistance to students.

    a. About how many undergraduates are receiving scholarships or other financial aid
        contributed by your college? Exclude assistance deriving totally or primarily
        from government funds.

              About _____ undergraduates 18-
                          (Number)

    b. About what is the total dollar amount of such aid from your college for the current
        academic year?

              About _____ dollars 19-

4. Does your college currently participate in the Federal government's "work-study" program?

    20-0 ☐ No

    1 ☐ Yes. About _____ undergraduates are beneficiaries 21-
                      (Number)

5. Does your college currently participate in the Federal government's national defense student loan program?

    22-0 ☐ No

    1 ☐ Yes. About _____ undergraduates are beneficiaries 23-
                      (Number)

           *   *   *   *   *   *   *   *   *   *

6. Colleges have various criteria for the acceptance or rejection of applicants. We are thinking of such things as local or state residence, high school standing, age limits, academic areas of interest, and so forth. Would you please check as many of the items on the following list as are relevant in the admission decision at your college--and also describe each item you check on the lines provided, telling us how each is applied? The following abbreviated example may serve as a guide:

EXAMPLE

Criterion	Description
☑ High school standing	Top half only are admitted
☑ Results of tests of ability	Top half only are admitted
☐ Local residence	
☑ State residence	Only 10% out of state are admitted
Et cetera	

Now please answer these:

	Criterion	Description
24-0 ☐	High school standing	_____
1 ☐	Results of tests of ability	_____
2 ☐	Local residence	_____
3 ☐	State residence	_____
4 ☐	Age	_____
5 ☐	Personal references	_____
6 ☐	Secondary school recommendations	_____
7 ☐	Academic areas of interest	_____
8 ☐	Achievement in non-academic areas, excepting sports	_____
9 ☐	Athletic ability	_____
25-0 ☐	Impressions from personal interview	_____
1 ☐	Financial need	_____
2 ☐	Relationship to alumnus	_____
3 ☐	Other criteria? (Please specify)	_____

278

7. What would you say is the one most important criterion for admission to your college?

    26- _____

    _____

8. Are there any particular types or groups of students your college is especially anxious to enroll?

    27-0 ☐ No

      1 ☐ Yes. What kinds? Check as many as apply.

        28-0 ☐ Students with unusually good secondary school records

          1 ☐ Students with unusual academic potential

          2 ☐ Students from socially or economically deprived backgrounds

          3 ☐ Students in the community where your college is located, or its immediate vicinity

          4 ☐ Students from the state in which your college is located

          5 ☐ Out-of-state Southern students

          6 ☐ Students from other parts of the country

          7 ☐ Foreign students (specify) _____

                    _____

          8 ☐ Athletes

          9 ☐ Other than Negro students

        29-0 ☐ Students especially well qualified in particular academic areas (specify) _____

                    _____

          1 ☐ Students with particular vocational objectives (specify) _____

                    _____

          2 ☐ Any other particular types or groups? (Specify) _____

                    _____

                    _____

9. (If "Yes" to Question 8) By and large, are the types or groups you checked in the last question as well represented in the student body as your college would wish?

    30-0 ☐ Yes

      1 ☐ No

QUESTIONS ABOUT RECRUITMENT OF NEW STUDENTS

Many colleges and universities devote considerable time and effort to the recruitment of new students. Others do not. We would like to ask you a number of questions relating to recruitment at your school. By recruitment we mean planned efforts to interest potential applicants in your college, above and beyond publication of traditional information materials, such as course catalogs.

10. a. Is there anyone at your college whose full-time job consists of recruitment of new students?

    31-0 ☐ Yes, self

    1 ☐ Yes, other person _____

    2 ☐ No   (His or her title)

b. (If "No" to 10.a.) Is there anyone for whom recruitment of new students is an important part of his or her official job?

    32-0 ☐ Yes, self

    1 ☐ Yes, other person _____

    2 ☐ No   (His or her title)

c. (If "No" to 10.a. and 10.b.) Who then does the recruitment? Check as many answers as are applicable.

    33-0 ☐ Nobody really does any (SKIP TO QUESTION 16, p. 6 - GREEN TYPE)

    1 ☐ Recruitment is usually part of the job of _____

        (Title of person)

    2 ☐ Various persons on the college staff work on recruitment, in addition to their teaching or other regular assignments

    3 ☐ Recruitment is chiefly done by the alumni or other friends of the college

    4 ☐ Our college is a public facility and recruitment consists primarily of efforts by public agencies outside the college

    5 ☐ Any other recruitment persons or agencies not listed above? (Specify)

    _____

11. Of what does your recruitment program consist? Check as many items as apply.

    34-0 ☐ Recruitment visits to high schools

    1 ☐ Organized recruitment efforts by alumni and other friends of the college

    2 ☐ Planned publicity for your college in the press or other communications media

    3 ☐ Periodic distribution of announcements of specific programs or offerings of your college to other schools or institutions, for posting on bulletin boards or general distribution

    4 ☐ Visiting days for secondary school students

    5 ☐ Scholarships or other financial aids for high school students you would like to enroll, excepting athletic scholarships

    6 ☐ Athletic scholarships

    7 ☐ Any other forms of recruitment? Please describe briefly.

    _____
    _____
    _____

12. a. We know it is difficult to say when such programs as planned recruitment at colleges began. Would you say, however, that by and large the program at your college was in effect prior to 1962, or did it start in 1962 or later?

    35-0 ☐ Prior to 1962   1 ☐ 1962 or later

    b. (If 1962 or later) Why was this program adopted?

    36- _____

13. Are there any particular types or groups of students which your recruitment program seeks to interest in your college?

    37-0 ☐ No

       1 ☐ Yes. What types or groups of students? Please check as many as apply.

          38-0 ☐ Students with unusually good high school records

            1 ☐ Students with unusual academic potential

            2 ☐ Students from socially or economically deprived backgrounds

            3 ☐ Students in the community where your college is located, or its immediate vicinity

            4 ☐ Students from the state in which your college is located

            5 ☐ Out-of-state Southern students

            6 ☐ Students from other parts of the country

            7 ☐ Foreign students (specify) _____

            8 ☐ Athletes

            9 ☐ Other than Negro students

          39-0 ☐ Students especially well qualified in particular academic areas (specify) _____

            1 ☐ Students with particular vocational objectives (specify) _____

            2 ☐ Any other particular types or groups? (Specify) _____

14. a. Have you expanded your recruitment program in the last three years?

    40-0 ☐ No

       1 ☐ Yes

    b. (If "Yes") Why do you think that this has occurred?

    41- _____

         _____

15. a. Do you expect expansion or intensification of your program in the next three years?

    42-0 ☐ No

       1 ☐ Yes

    B. (If "Yes") Why do you expect this?

    43- _____

         _____

Please answer questions 16 through 18 <u>only if you checked</u>: "<u>Nobody really does any</u>" (recruitment of new students) in Question 10.c. on page 4.

16. Why doesn't your college recruit new students? Check as many answers as apply.

44-0 ☐ We have as many qualified applicants as we can accept

1 ☐ Official regulations compel us to accept the great majority of secondary school graduates who apply

2 ☐ Official regulations limiting the activities of the college preclude a recruitment program

3 ☐ Such a program is against the general policy of this college

4 ☐ We do not have sufficient financial resources for a recruitment program

5 ☐ We do not have sufficient staff or staff time for a recruitment program

6 ☐ Any other reasons? _____

_____

_____

17. a. Do you feel that a recruitment program would be of value?

45-0 ☐ No

1 ☐ Yes

b. (If "Yes") Why do you feel this way?

46- _____

_____

_____

18. a. Does your college plan to start a recruitment program within the next three years?

47-0 ☐ No

1 ☐ Don't know

2 ☐ Yes

b. (If "Yes") What are the reasons for this decision?

48- _____

_____

_____

STUDENT INFORMATION FORM

Name of high school: _____   Location of high school: _____

Size of 1965 graduating class: _____ students. Number of graduates entering college this Fall: _____ students.

For each 1965 graduate entering college this Fall please enter data on a numbered line below.

Name of student	Sex	Name of college student will enter	Location of college: City or town	State	Class standing of student (top, 2nd, 3rd, or bottom quartile)	Ability or achievement test score (enter appropriately) Raw score	Natl. percentile norm	Please identify test: Name	Version (if more than one in use)
1.									
2.									
3.									
4.									
5.									
6.									
7.									
8.									
9.									
10.									
11.									
12.									
13.									

283

BIBLIOGRAPHY OF TEXT REFERENCES

BIBLIOGRAPHY OF TEXT REFERENCES

BOOKS

Becker, Gary S. Human Capital, A Theoretical and
    Empirical Analysis, with Special Reference to
    Education. New York: National Bureau of
    Economic Research, 1964.

Blumenfeld, Warren S. Some Characteristics of
    Finalists in the 1966 National Achievement
    Scholarship Program. NMSC Research Reports,
    Vol. 2, No. 2. Evanston, Ill.: National
    Merit Scholarship Corporation, 1966.

Clark, Kenneth B., and Plotkin, Lawrence. The
    Negro Student at Integrated Colleges. New
    York: National Scholarship Service and Fund
    for Negro Students, 1963.

Gordon, Edmund W., and Wilkerson, Doxey A. Com-
    pensatory Education for the Disadvantaged.
    New York: College Entrance Examination Board,
    1966.

Gurin, Patricia, and Katz, Daniel. Motivation and
    Aspiration in the Negro College. Ann Arbor:
    Survey Research Center of the Institute of
    Social Research, 1966.

Husan, Carolyn F., and Schiltz, Michael E.
    College, Color, and Employment: Racial
    Differentials in Post Graduate Employment
    Among 1964 Graduates of Louisiana Colleges.
    Report No. 116. Chicago: National Opinion
    Research Center, University of Chicago, July,
    1966.

McGrath, Earl J. The Predominantly Negro College
    in Transition. New York: Teachers College,
    Columbia University, 1965.

Roberts, Roy J., and Nichols, Robert C. Partici-
    pants in the National Achievement Scholarship
    Program for Negroes. NMSC Research Reports,
    Vol. 2, No. 2. Evanston, Ill.: National
    Merit Scholarship Corporation, 1966.

Tenth Annual Review of Research. Vol. 2, No. 11.
    Evanston, Ill.: National Merit Scholarship
    Corporation, 1966.

                ARTICLES AND PERIODICALS

Jaffe, A. J., and Adams, Walter. "Trends in
    College Enrollment." College Board Review,
    No. 55 (Winter, 1964-65), 27-32.

Jaffe, A. J., and Gordon, J. B. "A Note on Occu-
    pational Mobility for White and Nonwhite
    Males, 1950 to 1965." The New York Statis-
    tician, 18 (December, 1966), 1-3.

Moon, Rexford G., Jr. "A Model for Determining
    Future Student Aid Needs in the United States
    for the Support of Full-Time Undergraduate
    Education." Duplicated, 1964.

"Negro Higher Institutions in the South."
    Regional Action, 17 (June, 1966).

PUBLIC DOCUMENTS
AND GOVERNMENT REPORTS

Caliver, Ambrose. A Background Study of Negro
    College Students. Bulletin No. 8, Office of
    Education. Washington, D.C.: U.S. Government
    Printing Office, 1942.

Coleman, James S., et. al. Equality of Educational
    Opportunity. Washington, D.C.: U.S. Office
    of Education, 1966.

Fichter, Joseph H. Graduates of Predominantly
    Negro Colleges, Class of 1964. Public Health
    Service Publication No. 1571. Washington,
    D.C.: U.S. Government Printing Office, 1967.

U.S. Commission on Civil Rights. Racial Isolation
    in the Public Schools. Vol. 1, A Report.
    Washington, D.C.: U.S. Government Printing
    Office, 1967.

U.S. Congress. Senate. Committee on Labor and
    Public Welfare, Subcommittee on Education.
    Student Assistance Handbook. S. Doc. 26,
    89th Cong., 1st sess., 1965. Washington,
    D.C.: U.S. Government Printing Office, May,
    1965.

U.S. Department of Commerce. Bureau of the
    Census. "Educational Attainment: March 1966
    and 1965." Current Population Reports,
    "Population Characteristics," Series P-20,
    No. 158 (December 19, 1966).

_____. "Educational Status, College Plans,
    and Occupational Status of Farm and Nonfarm
    Youths: October 1959." Farm Population,
    Series Census-ERS (P-27), No. 30 (August,
    1961).

_____. "Factors Related to College Attendance of Farm and Nonfarm High School Graduates: 1960." Farm Population, Series Census-ERS (P-27), No. 32 (June 15, 1962).

_____. "Illustrative Projections of the Population of States: 1970 to 1985." Current Population Reports, "Population Estimates," Series P-25, No. 326 (February, 1966).

_____. Statistical Abstract of the United States, 1966. Washington, D.C., 1967.

_____. U.S. Census of Population: 1960. Characteristics of Teachers, Final Report PC(2)7D. Washington, D.C.: U.S. Government Printing Office, 1964.

_____. U.S. Census of Population: 1960. Detailed Characteristics, United States Summary, Final Report PC(1)D. Washington, D.C.: U.S. Government Printing Office, 1961.

_____. U.S. Census of Population: 1960. Educational Attainment, Final Report PC(2)5B. Washington, D.C.: U.S. Government Printing Office, 1963.

U.S. Department of Health, Education, and Welfare. Office of Education. General Studies of Colleges for Negroes. National Survey of the Higher Education of Negroes, Misc. No. 6, Vol. II. Washington, D.C.: U.S. Government Printing Office, 1942.

_____. Summary Report on Bachelor's and Higher Degrees Conferred During the Year 1963-64. Circular OE-54010-64. Washington, D.C., 1965.

ABOUT THE AUTHORS

A. J. Jaffe is Director of the Manpower and Population Program of Columbia University's Bureau of Applied Social Research and, since 1950, Lecturer in Sociology at Columbia University. Prior to his present position, he was a demographer at the U.S. Bureau of the Census, where he was concerned with manpower and demographic analyses for the United States and various foreign countries. He has served previously as consultant on manpower and population problems to the United Nations, to the Commonwealth of Puerto Rico, to the Republic of Panama, and to various public and private agencies in the United States.

Dr. Jaffe received his doctorate in sociology from the University of Chicago. He is co-author with Joseph Froomkin of Technology and Jobs (1968), author of People, Jobs and Economic Development (1959), co-author with Robert O. Carleton of Occupational Mobility in the U.S. 1930-1960 (1954), co-author with Charles D. Stewart of Manpower Resources and Utilization (1951), and author of Handbook of Statistical Methods for Demographers (1951). He has also written numerous monographs, reports, and technical articles on manpower, social insurance, and population.

Walter Adams is a Research Associate at the Bureau of Applied Social Research and has served with that organization for the past seven years. Prior to joining the Bureau, he was associated with several independent social research projects and a number of other research institutes, including the National Opinion Research Center, the New York City "School Health Survey," and New York University's study of foreign students attending college in this country. Mr. Adams has a master's degree from Columbia University.

Sandra G. Meyers is a Research Assistant at the Bureau of Applied Social Research. She previously was with the Center for the Study of Higher Education at the University of California. Mrs. Meyers is a graduate of the University of California at Berkeley.